SNACKS FOR THE BRAIN

By
Stephanie Foster

with admiration

Stephanie Foster

D1211278

Copyright © 1996 by Stephanie Foster
All rights reserved.

First Edition: November 1996

Book design and production by Joan Latture
Illustrations and cover design by Gayle McKennon

Portions of this text were originally published in the Harwich
Oracle and The Cape Codder

CAROUSEL
PRESS

PO Box 518
West Harwich, MA 02671

Manufactured on Cape Cod

FOREWORD

As you are about to discover for yourself, Stephanie Foster doesn't write about funny things. She writes about ordinary things as she sees them, and she sees most of them through the other end of the telescope.

The thing of it is, something comes under her scrutiny, and a sort of chemical change takes place. What looks like a simple rocking chair to you and me goes in rocking and comes out trotting.

This is why the condemned man, interviewed in his cell, said: "Give me that book by Stephanie Foster, and I'll die laughing."

Nothing so dire will happen to you. You'll just get a new slant on the everyday experiences of life.

But fasten your seat belt. A ride with Stephanie Foster takes some unpredictable curves.

If laughter is the best medicine, you'll never have a backache again.

> — John A. Ullman
> Author, and senior editor of
> *The Cape Codder*

Contents

JUST THINKING   1
Ears: Doorway to the Brain   3
Tooth or Consequence   5
Zucchini, the Landfill of Vegetables   7
Music: A Magical Trip   9
Dust Gets the Bum Rap   11
They Don't Chew on Slippers   13
This Is Your Warden Speaking   15
Love Your Dog? Take a Test   17
Your Shopping Cart Reveals All   20

SECRETS OF THE UNIVERSE   23
The Secrets of the Universe   25
Questions? Just Ask the Cricket Lady   27
Sailing Mumbo Jumbo   29
Menu, the Foreplay to Dining   30
Soft Fog to Embrace Cape   33
And Which Shell Has the Pea?   35
Facts: Snacks for the Brain   37
The Scales of Injustice   39
Born Without an Iron Hand   41
The Seven Pounds of Summer   43

WITHOUT RHYME OR REASON   45
Who Put the "Shhh" Signs Up in the Supermarket?   47
Tom, Dick and Larry Bird   49
Life and Death by Food   51
Close the Door on Cabin Fever   53
What to Give the Queen?   56
Tale of Two Sportsmen   58
His, Hers: Not Just Towels   60
It's a Retriever of a House   62
The Diet Pepsi Generation   64
She's No Longer Seeing Red   66

THEORIES AND THOUGHTS   69

Fat Attack   71

To Nap, or Not to Nap   73

The Ultimate Bad Hair Day Occurred
    a Long Time Ago   76

Is It Right to Be Wrong?   78

Man Came to Love His Lawn   80

Meltdown to Invisible   82

A Case of Selective Memory   84

The Lament of the Tongue   86

Rich or Poor, We Can't Forget Our Debts   88

English Has Become the Dagwood of Languages   90

Growing Up, Growing Older   92

OFF THE BEATEN TRACK   95

The Nose Knows Best   97

Training Toddlers for Space   99

Not All Is Gilded Fire Hydrants   102

Reflections of a Cave Bear   105

The Bungler's Cookbook   107

Let's Slice Our Own Cheese   109

All You Wanted to Know About Quarks   111

Refrigerators Very Revealing   113

Insider's Tips on Yard Sales   115

The Sirens of Winter   117

Truth About Easter Bunny Revealed   119

The Morphic Anomaly Principle   122

JUST
THINKING

EARS: DOORWAY
TO THE BRAIN

EARS aren't what they used to be. Oh, we still have them, but if we're not careful, they could go the way of the appendix—something we're born with, but never really use.

Remember the old westerns? An Indian scout would put his ear to the ground, then announce, "Nine horses, heading south, Kemosabe." Well, you don't see much of that anymore. and when's the last time you heard someone say, "Hark" or "Lo, someone's at the door"?

People used to be more ear conscious. They had lots of popular sayings like "Lend me your ears" and "In one ear and out the other." Even John Milton, who was no one to fool around, wrote, "I was all ears."

Ears were a pretty big deal before television was invented. Folks listened to the radio. People read to each other, told stories and had quiet conversations. In fact, they actually noticed the ear itself. Mothers despaired over infants with jug ears and tried to tape them down. Poets wrote about women's delicate little ears, comparing them to seashells. Pointed ears were considered a symbol of the devil and large ears, a sign of intelligence.

Life was simpler in the Time of the Ear. Ears blushed at compliments and burned when neighbors gossiped. Parents said, "Do you hear me?" and children did. But that was before heavy metal music. Now they turn a deaf ear.

Van Gogh even cut off his ear and sent it to his beloved. Cervantes claimed the walls had ears. Mothers everywhere clucked, "Did you wash your ears?" and old timers snickered, "You're still wet behind the ears," when someone was green and inexperienced. Everyone was either up to their ears in work or trouble.

Today, the ear is just another place to hang a decoration. Or attach a Walkman. Or rest a pencil. The rationale for fur earmuffs. A means of telling when you need a haircut. A handy location to attach eyeglasses or for bald people to grow hair. There are a few celebrity ears: Bugs Bunny, Dumbo and Mr. Spock. But who cares?

Nobody notices ears much nowadays. It's true they're sedate, non-moving body parts that don't show much expression, but that's not the reason. There are other parts of the body that have these same qualities and are adored. The reason nobody cares about ears, is that they are hard to observe on ourselves. So, we don't care what they look like on other people. Have you ever noticed that plastic surgeons never run ads for better looking ears?

Ears got shorted in the glamour department. There are no sayings like "Ears I could lose myself in," "Ears to die for," "Apple of my ears," "Drink to me only with thine ears," "Smoke gets in your ears."

Ears are not glitzy. They don't get starry-eyed. You can't bat your ears at someone, but they have other virtues. They're related more to the stomach than the heart. They digest things.

They don't drip, drool or make noise like some parts of the body. Ears are modest but have a good imagination. They are steady and constant. Unlike the eyes, they work while you're sleeping. Oh, one may be mashed into the pillow but the other one operates like a satellite dish listening for a baby's cry or a teenager creeping up the stairs.

Ears are not piggy or self-centered. They don't demand a Kleenex when you're at a movie or out walking on a cold day. They are pretty much upkeep-free. They don't bag or wrinkle. They don't need to be dyed, cut, curled or capped. And you don't have to match your wardrobe to them. Ears are a real bargain.

Like mittens, they work best in pairs. They can focus on a sound, the way eyes focus on an object, tuning in nearby conversation and tuning out an argument. They are stereoscopic.

Ears are not dazzling, merry or bright; they are the doors to the brain. If we were smart, we'd keep them open.

TOOTH OR CONSEQUENCE

I AM tilted back in the chair, but I can still read the Happy Tooth poster on the wall. I vow to never come back. In fact, I think I'll get out of here right now. Why not? I'm an adult; I have my rights. I can do what I want. It's my life. I don't have to put up with this.

The hygienist stares intently though her Darth Vader health mask into my open mouth. Her protective gloves smell of rubber.

"You know," she says, scraping the tartar from the backs of my teeth with a lobster pick, "You should be on a three-month recall."

"It's funny you should say that. . . ." She orders me to rinse my mouth with water. Disgruntled, I settle back into the chair and open my mouth like a baby bird expecting dinner.

"Close a little," she says. I reduce the opening. "That's better. These pockets around your teeth are pretty deep." She probes them with a steel ice pick to prove her point.

Scrape, scrape, scrape. She hits a sensitive spot, but I don't react. I give nothing away. Except I start to drool.

"Utt, guess we'll have to put this back in your mouth." Happily, she slips an ultrasonic drool controller in my mouth and it attaches itself to the nether side of my tongue like a leech. In seconds, my mouth is as dry as Phoenix. I am wondering if the thing can give me a hickey when she interrupts.

"Do you floss every day?"

"Well, ah, sometimes."

"You should, at least once a day and then use this," she says, holding a tiny Christmas-tree-shaped brush.

"I brush after every meal . . .," I say lamely.

"It's not enough. Actually, you brush too hard, that's why your gums are receding. Look." She holds a mirror up and my gums don't look happy like the ones in the poster.

A few minutes later, the dentist rushes in, washes his hands and turns to me with a big, white, happy toothed smile.

"Would you like gas, earphones, a Novocain or all of the above?" Cowardly, I opt for the Novocain. He stuffs cotton under my lip. "Open wide," he says. He is holding a giant needle behind his back.

This is it. I am never but NEVER coming back. The dentist hums to himself, oblivious of me and arranges his tools on a little tray. "Da, de da, de de da," he sings along with the radio.

When my lips feel as though they're bulging and my tongue and nose are asleep, he says, "I think we're ready." He turns the drill on: whine, crack, crunch, grind. "Seen any good movies lately?" he asks.

"Mmmrf . . ." I answer, so he tells me about his latest ski trip.

"Like to ski?" he asks.

"Dkrfin'ore."

He holds a glowing tube in my mouth. It looks like a prop from "Star Wars."

"Wha 'as kl'wn doin?" I ask.

"It's new—an ozone light wand. How's your husband?"

"Hiss 'ine.

"I'll be right back," he says and leaves me alone. I sit there quietly with my mouth ajar. My lips feel as though they are protruding and I glance down to see if they are sticking out. I notice a hand mirror next to the drill points on the little tray and pick it up to see if my lips look like they feel and am jolted by my reflection. I look like a primate.

"Lok't ma 'oth!" I say in alarm when he returns.

He looks at me, then removes the cotton stuffing from my mouth. Holding the mirror up, he says, "What do you think? Nice, huh." I bare my teeth at the reflection and notice that the dark, discolored filling is gone. It's been replaced by some kind of natural-looking material. I'm surprised at the improvement. "Make an appointment on your way out. We'll do the other one, next time," he says, smiling his happy tooth smile.

ZUCCHINI, THE LANDFILL OF THE VEGETABLE WORLD

A woman parking her car at the post office was approached by her neighbor, McDougall. "Gertie," he said, "Every time you come here, you lock your car. Are you afraid someone is going to steal it?"

"No," she answered. "I'm afraid someone is going to put zucchini in it."

* * * *

I AM spooning cream of zucchini soup into my smiling mouth. "Yum," I say. When I am through, the bowl is whisked away by my hostess and replaced with a cool summer salad. Forking through the greens, I discover the zucchini is cleverly disguised as cucumber.

"Delicious," I say to the host, looking around the table for more Thousand Island dressing.

A familiar odor precedes the large casserole dish being carried into the dining room.

"Umm," I say, sniffing, as the hostess unveils the dish. "What is it?"

"Poisson au bleu cockaigne," she answers proudly. "Zucchini stuffed with bluefish. I invented it myself."

I feel my throat tighten as I re-butter a slice of zucchini bread. The dessert is mock apple pie, but I don't ask any more questions.

Finally, it's time to go home. I resist the urge to rush; no need to panic, take it slowly. I wave good-bye and amble to my car. Calmly, I open the door and climb in. I am safe.

Suddenly my hostess shoots out the back door with a large brown bag in her arms and runs to the car before I can escape. "From our garden," she says triumphantly, pinning me to my car seat. My thighs are numb from the weight. Giant zucchinis stick out of the bag like green baseball bats.

"But I'm going away," I protest.

Her husband appears with a second bag. "Take some to your friends," he says, hoisting another 20 pounds into the window of my car.

My lips are wrestling for the right words. I start to squirm. I feel twisted, trapped. Eventually my eyes open and I am tangled in the sheets with the sun streaming into the room.

* * * *

What are we going to do with all the zucchini people are growing? Would V-8 Vegetable Juice consider becoming V-9? The challenge isn't growing it. It's getting rid of it. In the summer, zucchini is like beach sand; it is everywhere. The landfill of vegetables.

It's easier to give away a litter of kittens than zucchini. Unfortunately, it's not an addictive food. You can eat just one.

The Zucchini Institute has come up with some ingenious recipes, but it needs marketing help. A little sizzle to whet appetites. Look at the panache "Beefsteak" tomatoes have acquired and "Oyster" mushrooms. Peppers were languishing on the vine until someone came up with a brainstorm: a new palette of designer colors, purple, orange and yellow.

Maybe a new use would do it. A refreshing zucchini drink might be just the ticket. Something frozen with a wallop to it, like they serve in the islands. Nothing is impossible. If someone can invent a product called "Gatorade" or sell squid-flavored black pasta, we can do something with zucchini. All it needs is some favorable press, a health angle or New Age attribute.

The answer could be staring us in the face. The Zuccrannie. Ocean Spray doesn't have a cran-vegetable yet; it would be a perfect addition to its line.

Crossbreeding zucchini with cranberries would produce a luscious green vegetable the size of a gum ball. Cranzucs, maybe. Injected with protein and carbohydrates and served with milk, it could be a complete meal. Meanwhile, something has to be done. Zucchini is growing like a chain letter all over the country.

MUSIC: A MAGICAL TRIP

THERE are clear, sunny days that make you want to sing. And I do. Alone in my car. Aretha Franklin comes on the radio and we sing together.

"Chain, chain, chain,. (chain, chain, chain)
Chain, chain, chain, (chain, chain, chain)
Chain of fools, OHHHH,.
For five long years, I thought you were my man.
But I found out, I'm justa link in your chain,
OHHHH.
You got me where you want me.
I ain't nothin' but your fooL
You treated me mean, OHHHH,
You treated me crueL
Chain, chain, chain, (chain, chain, chain)"

I am thumping like crazy on the steering wheel. Windows down, sunroof open, what a day! The traffic rolls by and I wait my turn patiently. I feel free as a bird until I notice a couple of construction workers staring at me.

They expect to see a hot-looking blonde with hair flowing over her shoulders. Instead they see a middle-aged lady who looks like she's talking to herself, while music pulsates out the windows of her sedate gray compact car. They go back to work.

But they are wrong. I am a wild child. Hip and groovy. Styling. Chilling out. I have gone back in time.

"Dur wha ditty, ditty, dum ditty do.
Dur wha ditty ditty, dum ditty do
Here she comes justa walking down the street,
Singing dur wha ditty, ditty, dumm ditty do."

I am back in the '60s, a sweaty-palmed teenager, wondering why I cut my hair so short and thinking no one will ever ask me to dance again. Music can do that, lift you right out of your seat and plop you down somewhere else. Music makes memories bubble right out of your brain.

"Oh yes, I'm the Great Pretender.
Pretending that you're still around"

It is dim in the gym and I am wearing the lime green dress my mother made with the rick-rack around the collar, so it is just as well. Davie asks me to dance. We rock back and forth, feet firmly in place. He chews gum in my ear.

"Let's twist again like we did last summer
Let's twist again like we did last year."

Music is a space ship that hurtles me through time. I walk into a fraternity party. Couples are dancing wildly, frantically. I have never seen anything like it. How can they do that? It's so vulgar, but everyone is doing it. *"They call it the Twist and it goes like this."* I am shocked, but a month later I'm twisting. By then everybody else is doing The Monkey.

There were years of folk, rock, jazz, classical, blues and pop, then somewhere along the line, my musical tastes settled. Froze in place. Stopped advancing. Just as my parents rejected rock. I dismissed heavy metal. My mind is full of all the sounds it wants to know.

The eye is no friend to the past. Bodies age, neighborhoods shrink; nothing looks the way it used to. But the ear. Ah, the ear doesn't disappoint. It recalls simpler times, when problems were surmountable, and stress hadn't been invented. The ear is reliable. And music is magic.

"Dur wha ditty, ditty, dum ditty do."

DUST GETS THE BUM RAP

EVEN before women were hysterical about "ring around the collar," there was Dust Dread. I think the Pilgrims might have brought it over with them. My mother had a classic case. Each morning she would glide in and out of every room with a dust mop in her hands, then vacuum thoroughly on Saturdays. It's a trait that can skip generations, however, like having twins or eating in the dining room.

Sometimes I think I would rather move than clean. Instead of Dust Dread, I suffer from Good Intentions. This means I talk a lot about cleaning the house, but never actually do it. "The house is a mess," I tell my husband. "I'm going to stay home and clean. If you can't reach me, I've probably gone shopping for Dust-Off." Instead, I make a pie.

During the winter it's a snap to put off, with all the snow and mud being tracked in. Then, before a person can get organized properly to do a thorough spring cleaning, the pollen arrives. It is some kind of pollen. Before I came to the Cape, I knew nothing of pollen. I thought it was something bees collected and asthmatics suffered from. I didn't know it drifted into open windows like snow and camouflaged cars as if they were on an Army maneuver. I didn't know you were supposed to button up the house as if there were a hurricane outside.

I have nothing against pollen. It gives you a chance to see what your decor would look like if you had gone for green/yellow instead of rose/blue. And my husband and step-daughter can leave messages for me on the table tops. Oh, I swat at the window sills and walls, make a few lazy passes under the beds, but then give up. No one can be expected to fight millions of molting pine trees.

In the summer, dead mosquitoes stencil the walls and cat hair wafts from room to room like dandelion fuzz. No one notices because no one is home. "I'm going to clean," I announce, and then go out, too. Saying it makes me feel better.

When I moved out of the city, I figured my life would be cleaner but that was because I didn't have a complete understanding of dust. I thought it had something to do with city life and seeped in through the window casing while I slept. Now I know better.

Dust is everywhere. It is infinite and eternal. You do not get dust nor do you get rid of it. Dust is indigenous.

It's natural, organic and free. Maybe that's why it doesn't get much respect. People treat it as if it were a run in their stocking.

I think dust is getting a bum rap because people confuse it with dirt. Dirt is soil. Dust is a fine particulate matter made up of something that has disintegrated.

Dust is your life condensed to a powder. It comes from clothes dissolving and houses decaying around you. One day you'll look in your closet and your favorite blouse will be gone and there'll be a pile of dust in its place or maybe it will just be frayed or faded.

My husband doesn't agree with me about fading. I say, "It's the first micromillimeter of color sloughing off." He says, "Light causes fading." I say, "How does something fade in a dark closet?"

Have you ever wondered why antiques are so hard to find? Or where holes in socks come from? Or missing buttons go? They have bitten the dust.

This is not some kind of weird New Age View. Years ago, T.S. Eliot wrote:

> "Dust in the air suspended
> Marks the place where a story ended
> Dust imbreathed was a house
> thew all, the wainscot and the mouse. . . ."

Have you noticed that as people get older, they shrink and their house gets dustier? You lose a little part of yourself and your home when you clean too vigorously. It actually takes a lot out of you.

Occasionally I have stirrings of guilt about my mopless hands and remember the endless hours of cleaning my mother put in. But then, I think of the neat epitaph Dorothy Parker wrote for herself: "Excuse my dust."

THEY DON'T CHEW
ON SLIPPERS

THERE'S an organization that comes to the aid of collies in distress. It is quite a nice thing they do, these collie aficionados. If a collie is abandoned, abused or lost, they come and get it and find it a loving home. I think there should be a similar group for poinsettias. The Poinsettia Rescue League.

I am one of those people who should never be allowed to have a poinsettia. Oh, it's always fine in the beginning. I'll be at the supermarket or garden center and come across a display of them all huddled together and before I know it, I'm moving them around to find the biggest one to take home.

"What are you going to do with this plant after Christmas?" asks a small voice. It is the voice of experience.

"Shhh," I say. This year, it will be different.

For the first few weeks, the poinsettia gets the royal treatment. I shoo the cat away if he looks like he is even thinking of munching on a branch. The plant gets the prize window and I check it daily for moist soil and dry leaves.

Then sometime in January, things change. The Christmas tree comes down, I put the decorations away and the house settles down to its normal pink and blue. Except for the poinsettia.

"Want a nice poinsettia plant?" I ask friends and neighbors who drop by. "They grow wild in Mexico. Imagine." There are no takers.

I move it to a less desirable location and slowly begin to neglect it. It's all very subtle. I don't bother with plant food. I forget to water. The window shade stays down till dinner time.

What has this poor plant ever done to me? All it demands is a little attention. Why am I unconsciously plotting its demise?

Suddenly it looks too bright and garish. I don't want it anymore. But it's mine, a living thing and I'm responsible for it.

Secretly, I hope it will catch a cold. Or get root rot. I contemplate putting it out on the deck. Maybe all its leaves will fall off and I'll only have the stems to dispose of. I want it to shrivel up so I can justify putting it in the trash.

But no, the cunning plant thrives. It is a tough shrub that can withstand anything. It may get leggy or grow green leaves, but it lingers on. Nothing short of murder will get rid of it.

That's where the Poinsettia Rescue League comes in. Every February, they could pick up all the unloved poinsettias and place them in good homes where they'd be taken care of and nurtured 12 months a year.

The days are stretching out and soon it will be spring, with all its fragrant possibilities. Creamy lilies, golden daffodils, lavender hyacinth and soft pink tulips. Plants that symbolize anticipation and hope. And there's that darn poinsettia on the windowsill. A foreigner in the Easter landscape.

At least when spring flowers have gone by, you can plant the bulbs outside. And hope that they come up next year. You've had your pleasure and done your duty. It's more than fair.

Not so with poinsettias. The only good thing I can say about them is that they don't chew your slippers.

THIS IS YOUR WARDEN
SPEAKING

"**D**ID you measure that butter?" I ask my husband, eyeing the yellow glob on his plate.

"I estimated. It's probably under," he answers but I already have a measuring spoon in my hand.

"You can't guess. You have to be exact," I say, like someone about to check the length of a striped bass. "Well, that's a pretty good guess." I scrape the butter out of the measuring spoon and back on to his toast plate.

My husband is in Food Jail.

I am the warden.

"Three fats a day. That's all you get. Butter, mayonnaise, olive oil, it's all the same. And it's teaspoons, not tablespoons. You can blow them all in one meal or invest them wisely. I'd save them for salads if I were you," I say.

"What about my toast?" he asks.

"Don't have toast. Eat cereal instead," I advise.

It's not easy, this warden business. You need the wisdom of Solomon, the patience of Job and the authority of a federal judge.

The first morning was the worst. I carefully laid out breakfast: a half grapefruit, cheerfully festooned with a strawberry, and a bowl of Total with skim milk.

"Is that my cereal?" he asked.

"You have to get used to smaller portions. That"s three-quarters of a cup," I answered.

"What a cruel joke," says he. "When's lunch?"

We quibble. "Is your lamb chop bigger than mine?" he asks, leaning forward to see it better.

"It just looks bigger, yours is thicker," I answer and eat faster.

We fight. "Margarine is better for you than butter," I say.

"I'm not using it," he says. "It's nothing but chemicals and fat. People don't even know what it is. Remember Thalidomide. Years from now, you'll find out about margarine. Besides, I like butter."

We lie. "Did I hear you in the kitchen a minute ago?" I ask.

"I was getting some water," he answers. "What's that you're eating?

"Mmm . . . nothing. Apple," I say, swallowing. Wardens may have special privileges but they should never be flaunted in front of the prisoners.

Time passes slowly when you're in Food Jail. My prisoner waits for his meals like a baby bird, expectantly, helplessly.

But mostly he takes it like a man. He eats his grapefruit as if he were biting down on a stick—while a bullet was being removed. He is stoic. He is strong. Well, not all the time.

"I'm not going to stay on this diet if it makes me sick."

"Sick? It's all healthy food. Just less of it," I counter.

"There's too much fruit. I'm going to exchange an orange for a bread," he says.

"Wait a minute," I say. "Put that bagel down."

"My skin is itchy. It's the poisons coming out."

"What poisons? It's the weather. Everybody has dry skin. Besides, you've only lost 10 pounds," I say.

"I may not be able to diet next week. I'll be working out of town. I'll start again the following week," he says, resigned to his fate.

"Nonsense. I'll pack your lunch. Tuna or turkey with a nice salad and an apple," I say, refusing him parole.

He looks unhappy. "Well, we'll see," he says. Visions of pizza dance in his head.

"A diet is a lifetime thing. We have to change our eating habits forever. Get used to poached chicken instead of Kentucky Fried," I encourage. "Otherwise, your weight just yo-yos back and forth. It's not that you'll never be able to eat doughnuts or chocolate. You will, but in moderation."

The realization that my prisoner will be gone for a week has set in. I will be home alone. Fried haddock, French toast, cheeseburgers. . . .

LOVE YOUR DOG?
TAKE A TEST

I AM as crazy about animals as the next person. Well, maybe not as crazy as the Creightons next door. Their dog, Rusty, a sizable golden retriever, runs their life. He is a take charge dog. Dogs are pack animals with a pecking order and know instinctively that someone has to be at the top of the totem pole. Plus they figure they know more about enjoying life than we do.

Rusty is the head honcho over there. I know. I have walked this dog.

"No, Rusty," I say, "Don't go into the bushes." Sprong. My arm is pulled out of its socket. I am being dragged into the thicket. "No, Rusty, no." I say. He looks back over his shoulder at me and smiles. He thinks I'm really stupid. This is the best part of the walk; where the good smelling stuff is.

Rusty doesn't get away with this with my husband. One reason is that my husband speaks to him with authority. He has trained dogs before. "Rusty," he says in a loud, firm voice. The other reason is that he can give him a good yank. Rusty understands that my husband does not fall under his jurisdiction so he follows him amiably down the road. I have tried to master this technique.

"RRRR-usty," I say, trying to sound like Orson Welles. "Be a good doggie. Come back here."

Sixty seconds later, Rusty comes out of the woods, covered in mud up to his elbows, and shakes all over me.

I report to his owners. "Rusty rolled over a dead skunk. I couldn't stop him."

"Well, ha ha. That's all righty," they say, patting him on the head. "What'd ge do, gee good baby," they say, serving him a bowl of potato chips in his favorite chair.

I just read that Henry Kissinger walks his own dog, a black Lab, in New York City, where they have very strict pooper-scooper laws. His devotion ends there, however. A manservant follows behind him with the appropriate equipment to keep the streets tidy. I guess that's what the rich and famous do in the city.

Lately, I've been reading about the special feelings people have for their pets. Like the Florida woman who gave mouth-to-mouth resuscitation to her schnauzer after he bit a poisonous toad.

Of course, she didn't know it at the time. The dog was foaming at the mouth (which had turned purplish-brown) and shaking violently. Fortunately, she was a home care nurse. First she tried the Heimlich maneuver, but it didn't work, so she clamped the dog's nose shut and blew into his mouth, then pumped up and down on his chest. Later, the vet said it was definitely bufo marinus toad poisoning. Her quick action saved the dog's life.

The question is, would we have done the same thing if our dog had bitten a poisonous toad? That is, if we had thought of it. I know I probably wouldn't have thought of it myself.

One must keep in mind that a dog's mouth is supposed to be cleaner than our own, even though we don't go sniffing and licking the places and things they do. You probably know this already, but I thought I'd remind you.

While you are pondering the question, I'd like to mention something I read in an Annie Leibovitz interview. She is the famous photographer who takes pictures of famous people for famous magazines. Usually, she spends a lot of time with her subjects, getting to know them and cutting through all the phoney baloney. This way, she gets really interesting photographs.

Of course, she's seen a few unusual things. Debra Winger likes to kiss her dog on the mouth. Newsman Peter Arnett, who covered the war in the Gulf, goes a step further. He puts his tongue in his dog's mouth.

Are you still there? Ms. Leibovitz, who used to work for *Rolling Stone* magazine, called it special bonding with their animals. I am not calling it anything. I know there are people in this world who are revolted by the idea of using the same spoon for their coffee as is used to scoop cat food out of a can, after it's been washed, of course.

Now, I'm going to make a confession. I let my immaculate, white indoor cat, who does not sniff any of that stuff dogs sniff, share my bowl of cornflakes in the morning. I am telling you, just in case I become famous and Annie wants to photograph me. And also to let you know that I have a special bond with my cat.

So, what's your answer? I would perform mouth-to-mouth resuscitation on (choose one):

(a) My own dog, absolutely; (b) Your dog, but only if it had recently brushed its teeth; (c) Any dog whose will I was in; (d) I would call the Florida woman to perform mouth-to-mouth resuscitation.

Don't hurry. Take a little time to think about it. I am. (RRRR-usty, I'm only kidding!)

YOUR SHOPPING CART
REVEALS ALL

MY head swivels when I see a cart with a case of Twinkies and two gallons of Cherry Coke go by at the supermarket. I glance up expecting to see a malnourished food junkie with limp hair and bulging thighs. Instead, it's a tall, evenly tanned blond who looks like the captain of a world class rugby team. My own cart is full of whole wheat bread, fresh broccoli and yogurt and I'm the one with the Twinkie-freak body.

Cruising down the aisle, I wonder if I'll bump into rich dwarves filling their carts with miniature vegetables. Who else would pay $6.99 per pound for them. I fantasize about actually finding kohlrabi or bok chow in someone's cart. Every week, the stuff comes in by the truckload and is gobbled up by the knowing. If I could just observe a buyer or two, I might get an idea as to whether it should be served sunny side up or poached.

Usually, I linger in the produce department, hoping to catch someone decisively choosing between shitaki, chanterelle, oyster and the fourth in the species, the regular mushroom. In the past, I have mostly selected mushrooms by picking the ones with the least dirt. I admit I am nervous about trying the new ones. I can visualize my 10-year-old daughter isolating an oyster mushroom on her dinner plate as if it were a house fly.

"What's this, Mommy?" she'd ask, jabbing at it with her fork.

"It's a mushroom, Trudy," I'd reply "You like mushrooms."

"It doesn't look like a mushroom," she'd counter, pushing it to the limit of the plate.

"It's an oyster mushroom," I'd say.

"I hate oysters," she'd whine. "You know I hate oysters."

Calmly, I'd explain, "Well dear, it's not an oyster. They just call it that. It's a mushroom that . . . ah . . . looks like an oyster, sort of."

"I'm not eating it. You eat it."

Shopping carts contain more information about a person than astrological charts. I've seen the Tormented belly up to the checkout counter with diet cola, Sealtest Ice Milk and a pound box of double-stuffed Oreo cookies. The Determined buy cucumbers, skim milk and pita bread; the Elderly, individually wrapped slices of Kraft cheese, small loaves of Arnold white bread and Grapenut Flakes. The Yuppie has recently made an appearance with purple peppers, spaghetti squash, and designer herbs. This is the only shopper in the supermarket with elephant garlic breath.

Unfortunately, there is an inverse relationship between the pleasure of peering into someone else's cart and the pain of them peering into yours. I don't mind my neighbor checking out my horoscope in the paper every day, but I loathe the idea of running into her at the supermarket. One glance and she'll know I serve frozen generic peas, Duncan Hines brownies and still use my high school recipe for onion dip. Worst of all, my sweet tooth will be uncapped. She'll never believe I buy choco-mallow cookies for the dog or that I keep Skybars and Snickers on hand because Halloween has a way of creeping up on me.

Maybe carts should have darkened sides for privacy, like vans or limousines. I can't bear to be sniffed at by someone who lives on Bremmer crackers, goose paté and artichoke bottoms.

I could always shop in another town. But then I'd never know that the Smiths got a new puppy and Betty is back on Weight Watchers.

SECRETS
OF THE
UNIVERSE

THE SECRETS
OF THE UNIVERSE

I **DON'T** think the term "scientist" was presented to me properly when I was in school. I grew up thinking a scientist was a fussy, humorless person, who went around systematizing notes on 5 x 7 index cards to determine the nature or principles of something meaningful but obscure and who wore glasses and couldn't dance. I didn't realize they did interesting things like researching dinosaur flatulence.

I pictured people in white lab coats bent over petri dishes, talking to themselves: "Two million and one microorganisms; two million and two. . ." and making little stick-like marks on a pad of paper, until the phone rings and they have to start all over again. A scientist was someone who brought a peanut butter sandwich to the lab and then couldn't remember where he put it by lunchtime. Not someone who's right there measuring the amount of methane that enters the atmosphere when a cow burps.

Scientists are doing some fascinating work these days. Take the group that's analyzing 80-million-year-old dinosaur dung. Makes questions pop right up, even in the average brain. For instance, if a dinosaur is 100 feet long, how large is the sample they're studying? And how big were the feet of the scientist who stepped in it?

The most important question of course, is why are they hunched around this particular specimen from the past? The answer is not "Because it's there." This is not Mount Everest. No. The reason is they think dinosaur flatulence might have warmed the Earth, millions of years ago.

Do not shake your head as though I am crazy. According to the Associated Press, "The study suggests gas from dinosaurs helped maintain or warm the existing tropical climate during the late Cetaceous era, when flowering plants and plant eating dinosaurs proliferated."

After finding chemical signs of bacteria and algae in these dinosaur doughnuts, the scientist concluded that the dinosaurs digested their food by fermenting it. Like cows and sheep. Thus giving off methane, a "greenhouse gas" that traps solar heat in the atmosphere.

The concept is staggering. Particularly if you imagine yourself as a small plant-eating animal living in a popular dinosaur neighborhood. There you are, a turtle, quietly nibbling on a clump of grass and a few feet away, a few 55,000-pound dinosaurs have just finished breakfast.

"Who did that?" says one dinosaur, while the others laugh uproariously.

Now we know why turtles hide in their shells. And why man didn't appear for another 70 million years. He was waiting for the air to clear.

If all this were true, we could sure use a dinosaur, rigged up of course with an emission control device, to warm up the Cape in the winter.

Unfortunately, dinosaurs have gone the way of the Edsel. Besides, not all scientists agree with the theory. They argue and bicker just like regular folks.

"I wonder whether or not," says Eric J. Barron, a Penn State climatologist, "there were enough dinosaurs to make that substantial a contribution to atmospheric chemistry."

"There were too enough dinosaurs."

"Were not."

"Were too, acorn brain."

"Were not, fossil breath." At this point, they get out their 5 x 7 index cards and whack each other over the head.

"Want proof? I'll give you proof." A mastodonersaurus chip flies through the air. In science, they let the chips fall where they may.

QUESTIONS? JUST ASK THE CRICKET LADY

"The cricket's gone, we only hear machines"
—David McCord

YOU are probably asking yourself, "Is it the Cape, or has the whole world been inundated with crickets?" Well, now you can relax. The Cricket Lady is here to answer all of your cricket questions.

Crickets are found throughout the world, not just on boggy, foggy Cape Cod. The word comes from the old French, meaning, "creaker." The bugs themselves can be traced back to the movie, "The Last Emperor," where, as a child, the emperor is given a cricket in a little box, which he stashes in the seat of his throne. At the end of the movie, he finds it again. But given the length of the production, it is suspected that the original cricket was replaced by a stand-in. Now on to your questions.

Is it true that crickets make that chirping sound by rubbing their legs together?

No, no, no. Impossible. The only time a cricket can make a sound by rubbing his legs together is when he's wearing corduroy pants. By the way, only males chirp and they chirp for about 20 hours a day. Females find it quite attractive. Unless they're trying to get some sleep.

OK, how do male crickets make that sound?

They create the sound by rubbing their forewings together like fiddlers playing a violin. Although they don't "sing," they are able to throw their "voices," like a ventriloquist. They may sound like they are rubbing their forewings in the closet, when they are actually under the dresser.

Why do crickets stop chirping when you approach?

They think it's unseemly to rub their wings together in public. The Chinese keep crickets in private little cages. They use them as watchdogs. Sort of a reverse burglar alarm. When it's quiet, they call the police.

Are crickets lucky?

Yes. Unless you step on them. A dead cricket is considered to be an unfortunate cricket.

Have any crickets reached celebrity status?

Generally, crickets are retiring and don't seek the limelight. But Jiminy Cricket was an exception. He made it big and had his own dressing room with a star on the door. Most crickets despise wearing clothes, however, and prefer working on sound tracks for movies.

What do crickets eat?

In their natural habitat, they nibble grasses and sedges. In an abnormal habitat, they will make do with dust kittens, old shoes and wallpaper glue. Some have developed a taste for soiled clothing and will eat the gravy stain out of a tie.

Can crickets fly?

They can, but rarely do. They prefer a lively broad jump.

Due to some phenomena, crickets seemed to have reached biblical proportions on the Cape. Should we be fearful?

No. Although crickets belong to the same genus, Gryllus and order, Orthoptera, as locusts, they do not travel in large aggressive swarms.

Crickets are homebodies and prefer that their young grow up in the same back yard as they did.

Do they make good pets?

Yes. With their round faces, cheery dispositions and undemanding ways, crickets make a nice addition to the household. Unless you happen to pair two males together. Then they are as fierce as wolves.

What is the life span of a cricket?

A cricket is born into this world in the late spring and spends most of its life eating and chirping. During the mating season, the chirping is ardent and melodious, only turning sharp and challenging when another male approaches. As the days turn cooler, the chirping slows and females bury their eggs. With the first autumn frost, they pass on to cricket heaven. All is silent. Then in spring, the next generation of tiny musicians begins its concert.

SAILING MUMBO JUMBO

ONCE upon a time, sheets were something I slept on, combing was what I did to my hair and JIB was the name of a radio station. That was BTB. Before The Boat. Now, instead of saying, "Yes, dear," I say, "Aye, aye, Captain."

I knew it was coming. My husband had been talking about The Boat for 10 years. That's how long it took to build it. I listened patiently the way you do when someone talks about UFOs or The End being near. Then one day, suddenly, in the time it takes a hen to lift herself off a nest, there it was—a fully hatched sailboat.

My husband is the ruler of this floating fiefdom. He even speaketh a new language to go with his new empire that I don't understandeth.

What I have observed to be a kitchen for most of my life is now called a galley. Leave it to a man to give a sink and a stove a macho name. I always thought galley had to do with printer's proofs or a form of slavery. The word seems to fall somewhere between a shooting gallery and the gallows. I think he enjoys saying, "She's down in the galley."

How can a room, whose function so obviously deals with the opposite end of the body, be called a head? I am learning that aboard a boat, most things do not look like their names. I could stare for half an hour and not see a shroud right in front of me.

Why is everything so complicated? There's True Wind, Relative Wind and Apparent Wind. Even weather forecasters don't talk that way. Does a landlubber call one end of their shoelace, the standing part and the other, the bitter end?

I think all this sailing mumbo jumbo is an effort on the part of men to confuse women and keep them in a subservient role. On a boat, normal words mean something else. A knot can be a nautical mile per hour, or a clove hitch, bowline or figure eight. Rope is rope until it's on a ship; then it becomes line. Our cockpit is so loaded with line, it looks like a bowl of spaghetti. We should have called the boat, The Linguini.

It's a good thing my husband hasn't asked me to trim the sails. I think I'd do them in pink and aqua. Why is it that a journal is a log and a map a chart? Wouldn't you think the line opposite the outhaul would be an inhaul instead of a downhaul?

Why is down, below? Why do they have to say fore and aft? I have always been bad at directions, responding slowly to the words right and left, and tending to gesture to one when I mean the other. For me, square dancing is a contact sport. Now I have port and starboard to contend with and it has tripled my response time. You'd think the port side would be the side you could see land from or where you kept the liquor. When my husband tells me to get something from the starboard side, I stand there like someone trying to conjugate a Latin verb.

Recently, my husband told me to untie the bumpers, excuse me, fenders from the stanchions. He gave me that steady look you give a dog when you hope they'll understand what you're saying from the inflection in your voice. "Get the newspaper, Rusty. The N-E-W-S-P-A-P-E-R." After a brief search, I recognized the fenders.

"Now stow them in the Lazarette," he continued. The only thing I could picture was the guy who rose from the dead. It's all very unsettling. I wonder if Berlitz teaches this stuff.

MENU, THE FOREPLAY
TO DINING

THERE are those who love to read romance novels or science fiction, but a well-written menu is my kind of literature. A menu can inspire awe, suspense and intrigue. And unlike a lot of books, there's usually a happy ending.

A menu can transport you to distant lands, introduce you to exotic dishes or show you how the other half lives. For me, menus are made to linger over.

My husband, on the other hand, thinks the Evelyn Wood Speed Reading Course was designed with menus in mind. He is the Sterling Moss of menu readers. It's like a flag drops when he is handed a menu and he is racing in the Indianapolis 500. Va-room he goes up and down the columns.

Meanwhile, I slowly unfold my napkin, glancing around casually at my fellow diners, noting what is on their plates and how far along they are in their meals.

My husband comes to a screeching stop on page two. "Guess I'll have the Sole Menemsha and um, the clam chowder," he says. "What are you having?"

"I don't know," I say, reaching languidly for my water glass. "I haven't looked at the menu yet."

My husband thinks eating out has to do with the food. He hasn't spent an hour getting dressed. He wants to get right to it.

"Look at that couple over in the corner. They must be from out-of-state. He's wearing argyle socks and a silk pocket hanky," I say, using diversionary tactics.

"Hmmm," says my husband, glancing vaguely in their direction. "I wonder where our waiter is."

"Does this place look like it serves really crisp duck? Or do you think it will be greasy?" I ask, finally reading my menu. "Fresh grey sole, topped with Nantucket scallops, morels, julienne snow peas and carrots with sauce Chardonnay. Yum."

My head swivels as a waiter goes by with a platter in each hand. Something with marinara sauce and melted cheese. I can't quite make it out, but the fragrance of it lingers. I swallow. There should always be a certain amount of mouth-watering foreplay before the actual act of ordering food.

I read the entire menu, cancelling out things I cook at home like chicken or anything poached, which is a terrible fate for any food.

Every now and then I scan the room in a studied, bored way, as if I'm not really paying attention. Actually, I am checking to see how the people around me like their food. I wait for the chew, the swallow and the reaction. Are they happy? Are they holding their forks up in a smile, or pointed down in a frown? Are they ummm-ing to their dinner companions or complaining? Is the waiter returning empty, licked-clean plates to the kitchen or half-full ones?

I hide behind my menu during my surveillance, but a woman eating a creamy piece of cheesecake catches me watching her. I smile encouragingly. It's almost as good as eating it myself.

The dessert cart is wheeled by our table and I falter, Creme broulé or a fruit tarte? I have to re-program my choices working backwards from dessert.

When the waiter comes back, I try to muster as much dignity as I can. "What comes with what?" I ask him. I don't want to order a salad or vegetable if they come with the meal.

"Do you think the Veal Oscar is a better choice than the Shrimp Portofino? What do you recommend? Were those crab cakes that just went by? They look delicious. Maybe you'd better give me a few more minutes."

Finally, I sip my wine and gnaw happily on a piece of bread.

"Have you decided?" asks my husband.

"Yes," I say, passing him my closed menu.

"Well?" he says.

"I'll have the same thing as you."

SOFT FOG TO EMBRACE CAPE

"Weather forecasts are only a recent invention. From the dawn of time until a hundred years or so ago, men relied on watching the clouds and memorizing verses to make their predictions of what tomorrow's weather will be."
— *The Weather Wizard's Cloud Book*

IT'S time to do something about the weather on Cape Cod. No more rolling over on our backs and putting our paws in the air. All it will take is a little initiative, cooperation and perhaps a tiny bylaw prohibiting the forecasting of bad weather. The climate, if you will, is right for it.

Tut, tut, the idea is not as preposterous as you think. Didn't the Pentagon impose restrictions on press coverage of the war in the Gulf? For security reasons? Well, we could do a similar thing with our weather forecasts for security reasons—economic security.

Tourism, like oranges and grapefruit, is affected by the weather. It's our cash crop, so to speak. We have to farm for all we're worth during the growing season. The mere threat of bad weather can ruin our harvest.

A droning forecast of intermittent rain goes beyond our purse strings. It affects our attitude. "Oh crumb, I just washed the car," men say. "Heaven help me!" say mothers of small children. "Wake me when it's sunny," say teenagers.

I am not proposing that we issue false weather reports. No. That would be dishonorable and possibly illegal. I am simply suggesting that we accentuate the positive.

Why do we have to say, "Chance of showers"? Does the State Lottery Commission mention "chance of losing," when you buy a Megabucks ticket? Of course not! They talk about happy things like winning money. They promote the positive.

Must we use phrases like, "unstable air masses"? Most people listen to forecasts by rote, the way they sing the national anthem and don't understand what the words mean anyway. The problem is the lingo sounds ominous. We need to use words that bring hope and joy. "Possibility of a gorgeous day," not, "chance of precipitation."

Can't we have "full shade at the beach" instead of "cloudy"? If it isn't a good day for biking, swimming and sunbathing, can't we suggest an afternoon at the movies, museums or malls?

We don't need a blackout on bad weather, just a positive perspective. What's so wrong with a dapple-gray kind of day? Weather can be uplifting, poetic even: A soft fog will embrace the Cape today. The air will be drenched in dew. Look for a dove-colored sky.

Let's get rid of the meteorologists with their tedious weather maps and satellite forecasts. I say we should have uncomplicated weather, the kind of weather we used to have years ago when people chanted:

> *"When white clouds cover the heavenly way*
> *No rain will mar your plans that day."*
>
> or
>
> *"Red skies in the morning, sailor take warning.*
> *Red skies at night, sailors delight."*

Why not say, "It's going to clear." We don't have to say when. High pressure, low pressure, how about a no pressure weather report? We need a new glossary of terms. "Gauzy" sounds better than cloudy. "Rainbow alert" is more interesting than rain. And "wave-watching spectacular" has it hands down over northeaster.

Suppose we gave a good weather report and it rained, what's the worst thing that could happen? Nothing. Right? Because everyone knows the weatherman is the only person who is constantly wrong and still keeps his job. We have nothing to lose.

And, if we had the right attitude, we could make rain out to be a mystical, rare event like snow in Florida. A reason to be jubilant. "Oh rare and mysterious rain from whence life's force is nourished; oh bringer of growth, refresher of lawns, cancel-er of window washing, we rejoice in your bounty. . . ."

Folks in Maine might think we're a little tetched. "Hear them Cape Codders dance in the streets when it rains, Mabel." But think of it this way: they have to live with bad weather.

AND WHICH SHELL
HAS THE PEA?

ven when I was a kid, I'd get sucked in. There'd be some magical Captain Marvel-type ring advertised on the back of a box of Wheaties and I'd send away my week's allowance. Six weeks later, it would arrive in the mail. I'd tear the packaging open and a dull, lifeless, worthless piece of plastic would fall out.

My dreams of intergalactic communication would fade. "I told you not to waste your money on that stupid thing," my mother would say, speaking in The Voice of Experience. I would shuffle off to my room and vow to never be so gullible again.

* * *

"It's a lifetime knife," says the guy at the Home Show. He is slicing tomatoes like a Vegas blackjack dealer; he pares an apple in a split second; carrot chips fly around him like speeding bullets. I am mesmerized. "And it can cut through anything." He reaches for a beer can and guillotines it.

My mind is like a back seat driver trying to jam on the brakes. No, Nooooo, it is saying. It flashes a vision of Ed McMahon on my mental screen. He is telling Johnny Carson about how he used to sell Veg-O-Matics when he first started out. He is laughing. They are both laughing. "How much does this Magic Lifetime Knife cost?" asks the man who resembles Ed McMahon, vaguely.

"$25? $20? You can't even buy this knife in a store. If you could, it would cost $15. But, I'm offering it to you, for today only, for only $5.95. That's right, $5.95."

I try to turn away, but there's a murmur in the crowd and everyone seems to be searching in their pockets for money.

"And that's not all, folks. As a special introductory offer, I'm going to throw in this wonderful Citrus Spritzer, absolutely free to the first 20 customers!"

He inserts the Citrus Spritzer into a lemon, then squeezes it. The juice squirts neatly out of the funnel into a bowl.

"No more mess squeezing lemons and limes when you have this miraculous gadget in your kitchen. You can use it on grapefruit, you can use it on oranges, you'll wonder how you ever lived without it. And you can't buy one anywhere. The only way you can get one is free, when you buy our Magic Lifetime Knife for only $5.95!"

The crowd starts to push forward.

"All this for only $5.95. Hurry before we run out!"

I find myself wiggling and pushing with the rest of the crowd, waving a bill in my hand. I'm not sure I need a lifetime knife that can cut anything but I sure want that citrus thing.

Mercifully, they don't run out before I can pay for my prize. Fresh orange juice every morning. Lemonade. I can't wait to try it. On the way home, I stop for lemons.

Dinner can wait. I screw in the Citrus Spritzer and squeeze. The juice runs down my fingers and onto the cuff of my sweater. I unplug it and try the other end of the lemon. The juice oozes around the opening and drips on the counter.

I squeeze harder. Nothing. I am out of juice. I take the spritzer out and inspect it. It looks like three cents worth of plastic.

I turn to the Magic Lifetime Knife. Up close, it is not very attractive and feels springy, like a cheap steak knife. I cut the lemons in half successfully. I survey the kitchen for a more serious challenge and saw off the top of a box of pasta. It takes me about two minutes and my husband asks me what I am doing.

"Watch this," I say, reaching into a bag of empty bottles for a beer can. Before his very eyes, I decapitate a can of Bud with much vigorous and determined sawing.

"Well?" he says.

"Well, what," I say, putting the knife in the drawer with my Captain Marvel ring.

FACTS: SNACKS FOR THE BRAIN

OME columnists, desperate for a topic, resort to writing about their cat or stories in the supermarket tabloids. Not me. My mind is as busy as a beehive with thoughts swarming around it constantly.

For instance, did you know that most people only brush their teeth for 30 to 60 seconds? To have healthy teeth and gums, you should do it for five minutes. The only time I brush my teeth for more than 60 seconds is on the morning I have a dentist appointment. Obviously, there's a market for a new product here. An interplac-WaterPik toothbrush with a built-in timer and web site.

Now that summer is gone and the air is cooler, I'm getting nervous. The average winter weight gain is 7 pounds. Even worse, the divorce rate rises in the winter because couples are cooped up together. If Ivana and Donald couldn't make it, rattling around in their Trump Tower mansion, what chance do the rest of us have?

I love tidbits of information; they're like snacks for the brain. Easy to digest. Plus they suit my childlike attention span and billboard mentality.

Sex can relieve arthritis pain (but it gives some women headaches). See? Some information is definitely easier to remember than how to read a tide chart and whether you add or subtract 25 minutes for each whatever-it-is.

Only 1 to 2 percent of adults have food allergies, yet up to 40 percent believe they have one. My step-children claim they are allergic to bluefish and spinach. I understand. I used to be allergic to turnip and cold peas, but I got over it.

The post office returned more than $40 million in tax refund money to the IRS in 1988 because taxpayers moved or gave faulty addresses. An info-bite like this leaves you hanging: then what happened to the money?

A good tidbit can impart insight into a previously unrecognized problem. To find your car in a crowded parking lot, buy a helium balloon on a string and tie it to your bumper or antenna. It can also stimulate thought: Where do you find a helium balloon in a crowded parking lot?

Taxpayers won only 5 percent of the cases filed against the IRS in tax court in 1988. (Was this information leaked to the public by the IRS to let us know what our chances are?)

A government committee in Finland has recommended that Finnish adults have sex more frequently to reduce stress. (Do they have a national campaign called, "Just Say Yes"?)

Simple statements can be quite provocative. For warmer hands in cold weather keep your neck covered. Now answer the following quiz: wearing mittens will make your neck: a) cold; b) warm; or c) confused.

Breast milk can be left at room temperature for up to six hours with very little risk. This is very good news for nursing mothers who find the refrigerator uncomfortable and chilly.

A thought-provoking statistic can be a good opening for cocktail party conversation. The maximum life span of an eastern box turtle in captivity is 138 years. Saltwater fish are no higher in sodium than freshwater fish. Twenty-six Eskimos live in Nebraska. Stutterers don't stutter when they sing.

With my luck, someone will probably want to talk to me about their cat or the latest tabloid story.

THE SCALES OF INJUSTICE

"**H**OW much do you weigh?" Luciano Pavarotti, the substantial Italian tenor, was asked that question at a news conference. He refused to answer. "I have lost 80 pounds and so I am 80 pounds less than I was."

It's the kind of answer my best friend would give. She'd rather reveal her net worth than her weight. It's a heavy subject. My husband teases her unmercifully by saying he can tell how much she weighs simply by lifting her up. She titters and squirms like a teenager when he pretends to try. Then he scrutinizes her like a county fair huckster.

"I bet I can guess within two pounds just by looking." She can't bear the thought and covers her ears.

At Weight Watcher weigh-ins, they card the front of the scale so people behind you can't see what you weigh. Why are those three numbers so painful and important? You'd think people would care more about their IQ. Actually there are two delusions about weight today that nobody talks about.

The first is the myth that one does not look like what one weighs, (hence the reluctance to tell the naked truth). The other is the "does this make me look thin?" fable. Both are wishful thinking.

We think we can disguise our figures by camouflaging them in dark colors with stripes going in the right direction or avoiding polka dot pockets on the hips. It's as if our shapes were a secret known only to ourselves. It's as if we truly believed that 165 pounds looks like 135 when properly cloaked. You can see how ridiculous this is if you try to do it with an inanimate object like a living room chair. No matter how you drape it, you know there's a stuffed chair in there somewhere.

I'm not funny about my weight. I can deal with the naked truth. I just have a few rules. The best time to weigh yourself is after a haircut and before a coat of nailpolish. All clothing, shoes, jewelry, watches, headbands, barrettes and bobbypins must be removed. Preferably, legs should be shaved, toenails trimmed and teeth flossed. Only idiots would weigh themselves after they shower. Skin is porous and has a tendency to retain water. Never weigh yourself if you have eaten anything. If you forget, put it off for another day. The ideal moment is first thing in the morning, before coffee and after elimination.

When making the approach to the scale, it is important not to jiggle it. Abrupt movements, jouncing or stomping on the scale, can cause the needle to barrel right past your true weight and never come back. The best method is to lower yourself slowly onto it, while gripping the wall with one hand. Hold your breath and release your grip at the last second.

It is perfectly acceptable to stand lightly on the scale with your heels dangling off the back, as long as both feet are off the floor.

It is permissible to factor in an accuracy equation of Minus Five Pounds because not all scales are that accurate—particularly on oppressive damp days. Scales are just as temperamental as cars. They have their ups and downs. Humidity can also hang on you, creating extra weight.

In addition, each person must review their own individual body traits which weren't taken into consideration when they made up those Recommended Weight Charts. Bone structure was taken into account but not things like shoe size. A person wearing dainty size sixes could weigh the same as someone with a nine-and-a-half wide but they wouldn't look the same. I know lots of people who carry their weight in their feet. So ask yourself the following five questions:

1. Is my hair thicker or longer than average?
2. Do I still have my appendix and tonsils?
3. Do I have large teeth or more than three fillings?
4. Am I a tall person with a short forehead which puts me in an unfair height category?
5. Since muscle weighs more than regular flesh, am I due a credit here?

Using this format, deduct from one to three pounds for each "yes" answer. When you take everything into consideration, you'll be able to deal with the naked truth.

BORN WITHOUT AN IRON HAND

THE world is divided between people who can iron and people who cannot. It either comes to you naturally or not at all, rather like the person who is mechanically inclined or can carry a tune. Many good ironers were child prodigies. If the truth be known, you have to be born to iron.

After years of struggling, I finally realized I will never be any better at ironing than I am at tennis. At first, I thought I was just a slow starter. My mother, a gifted ironer, never taught me to iron as a child. While other 12-year-olds were eagerly learning, I'd be out playing, humming tunelessly to myself. I assumed ironing would be like playing the piano—with practice, you'd move from "Chopsticks" to Chopin. I was wrong.

Nothing can prepare you for the leap from a table napkin to a long-sleeved shirt. How do you practice something you can't do? How does one progress from a bellyflop to a Flying Dutchman?

I remember pondering my first blouse. I still ponder. Do you begin with the collar or do you iron from the bottom up? How do you press the sleeves so they don't stick together? Do you iron around a dirty spot? Or over it? No one ever discusses it. Ironing tricks are guarded as closely as the Coca-Cola formula.

Last fall, I had to look impeccable at a book reception. I was the author's wife and people would be looking me over pretty closely. After rooting around in my closet, I found an ensemble from my trousseau that still fit. It was teal blue linen with a matching duster. Very Jackie O, but with wrinkles. All I had to do was iron it.

If they held ironing bees, linen would be the fabric they saved till last. They'd weed out all the neophytes and when they were down to the last two contestants, they'd bring out the linen.

I heated up the iron and began my task of relocating the wrinkles; they slowly spread from one place to another. Ironing the same spot over didn't seem to help it twice as much. I decided to risk a little spray starch. The fabric darkened under my onslaught and got worse when I pressed it. Ten minutes later, it was still dark and splotchy. I had ironed my dress to death with Spray 'n Wash. I wore the corpse and spent the evening locking eyes with anyone who looked my way, so they wouldn't notice the stains. That night, I renamed my iron "The Terminator."

During the zenith of my cotton craze, I bought sheets that had to be ironed. "Zero polyester," I crowed, until they came tumbling out of the dryer, engulfing the ironing board, the cat's litter box and every square inch of the laundry room. Now, every time I change the linen, it looks as though I'm holding a parachute-folding class.

Dedicated ironers are a breed apart. They have tidy hair and wait by the dryer for the buzzer to go off. Then, they either iron the laundry to a crisp, while it's still warm, or store it in the refrigerator.

Non-ironers think crisp is an adjective for food. They are immune to buzzers and don't take their laundry out of the dryer until it has stiffened to a state of rigor mortis. Twenty-seven days later, they iron. Once they go through menopause, they buy wash-and-wear fabrics and never iron again.

Those of us who constitute this minority shouldn't be ashamed. Many famous people were terrible ironers: Gypsy Rose Lee and Esther Williams, for instance. Instead of living a lonely, guilt-ridden life, we should unite. Come out of hiding. Form neighborhood support groups. Hold seminars. Network. Create a newsletter. Demand make-up and hairstyles that complement and enhance our disheveled look. It's time to come out of the closet, linen or otherwise. Everyone else has.

THE SEVEN POUNDS
OF SUMMER

IF you are built like Cher, or have never broken a zipper trying to squeeze into a pair of pants, please move on to another page. I mean it. Go eat a carrot. You won't understand today's subject.

Here it is Aug. 14 and I'm still waiting for my seven pounds to melt away—the seven pounds your average body loses each summer and gains each winter. I have never noticed this phenomenon happening to me, so I thought I'd pay attention this year. Well, actually I've been aware of the winter part, where you gain the weight, but not the other end, where it disappears.

Could the experts who came out with this statement have missed certain areas when they were weighing in the populace to get these statistics? Perhaps the study was limited to New York City, where whole bodies disappear in the summertime. Or maybe they examined people across the southwestern states and north and east into the Rockies and the Great Plains, where temperatures exceed 100 degrees Farenheit and folks give up pork rinds.

In the summer, New England has to be one of the greatest eating capitals of the world. Steamers, lobsters, corn dripping with butter, fish chowder, blueberry pie and vanilla ice cream.

When I say, "I couldn't eat another thing," there's a good reason. It doesn't mean I'm not hungry; it means I'm full.

I have heard some people say that they are too tired or too hot to eat. Not me. Nor am I ever too sad or too happy or too excited. I am always in the mood for food. My appetite never takes a vacation.

Summer is fried clam stands, cookouts, picnics on the beach, backyard barbecues and having maple walnut ice cream drip down your elbow.

Summer is not celery sticks and hard boiled eggs.

Summer is cool sea breezes, salt air and a hearty appetite.

Feeding friends and eating outside. Fried chicken and peach shortcake. Onion rings and Ring Dings. Fat tuna sandwiches, plump Dove Bars. Summer is lush and lazy.

Who has the energy to diet? Friends do not get together between meals and sit around with their hands folded in their laps. They celebrate the season with food. Everywhere I look, people are eating. In their driveways, on their porches, at the beach, in sidewalk cafes, outdoor restaurants, strolling along the street. They don't need a seat to eat. In the shade or sun or under the stars. With candles or without. Eat, eat, eat. Where are the sleek people with no appetite who are losing those seven pounds?

Dinner parties, clambakes, cookouts. Fast or fancy food. I'm surrounded. At every minute of any day, someone, somewhere is eating wherever I look. Ice cream cones, hot dogs, pizza, hamburgers, potato chips or fries, salt water taffy or fudge, submarine sandwiches, chocolate chip cookies. Street Food. It boggles the eye.

A resort community is a landmine of temptation. A body can hardly go to the post office or gas station without working up an appetite. We're embraced by a living menu.

Every night, I lie in bed, unable to move. "This has got to stop," I say. In the morning, I'm hungry again. Corn sells for nine cents an ear; lobster prices drop, more friends call to say they're coming. I make beach brownies, potato salad, company desserts. I eat as though every day is my vacation. For 12 weeks.

Fruit? Oh sure, fruit is fine. I make turnovers, pies and pastries, then add Ben & Jerry's finest. Fish? Fish is terrific, baked with a rich stuffing or topped with a butter-dill sauce. How can anyone possibly lose seven pounds during the summer when it is their duty to appreciate the bounty of the land and sea?

Soon summer will be over. The words "back-to-school" are already creeping into conversations. Restaurants will close and house guests will depart. The Food-A-Thon Season will be over. It's strange to think that that's when most of the country begins to gain weight.

WITHOUT
RHYME
OR REASON

WHO PUT THE 'SHHHH' SIGNS
UP IN THE SUPERMARKET?

HAVE you ever noticed the uncanny silence in those super supermarkets that are the size of Rhode Island? At least 152 women are shopping at the same time and no one talks. They wander up and down the aisles like pigeons following a trail of bread crumbs. It's eerie.

Who among us would dare ask a fellow shopper if the yellow peppers taste like bananas and if they're worth $6.99 per pound. There is no easy locker-room camaraderie where a person can turn to another and say, "I give up, what do you use the bok choy for?" Or, "Which does the elephant garlic taste like?"

It's as if we're in a library, looking for books. The only human sounds we hear come from unabashed children squealing at the brightly colored boxes on the bottom shelf, then their mother's hoarse whisper to, "put the Chocomallows back." Even when a toe is run over or a foot stepped on, the injured party smiles politely. It's as if we were in church. Is this normal?

No one hums to the "white sound" of the Muzak. Shoppers glide by row after row of canned goods in a trance. It's like a local production of "The Stepford Wives" with unseen people holding up huge "Shhhh" signs off camera.

When a label reader blocks the path, does a shopper ask the person to move? No. She waits mutely until the blocking party decides whether to use Zip or Zap in her laundry or checks to see if the ash content in Bonkers is too high for her cat.

Even if a person misplaces her cart, it is a silent affair. When you see a driverless cart parked somewhere between the sweet pickles and the stuffed olives, it is because someone had to double back for mint jelly, and has forgotten where she left it. Does she march up to the manager and ask for help? No. She searches around alone for 20 minutes, then goes home.

Eyebrows are raised but not voices when the ultimate breach of supermarket etiquette occurs—the taking of someone else's cart by mistake.

Occasionally, I'll find myself putting a half-gallon of Nuform into a cart heaped high with Frosty Bears and unsalted Saltines. I go into shock. It's as if someone has stolen my pocketbook and replaced it with another. While I'm thinking, "I've never eaten a Frosty Bear in my life," a disgruntled woman comes up and snatches her cart away from me. She acts as if I couldn't help myself, her cart looked so good to me, I had to have it for myself.

I am speechless as the miffed one sorts through her Fig Newtons and Gatorade to be sure I haven't stolen anything, or worse, left some disgusting thing behind.

While I am drafting my apology in my mind, she gives me a withering look and whisks her cart away. Meanwhile, eyewitnesses white-knuckle their own carts and stare straight ahead as if they hadn't seen a thing. I'm lucky to escape without being photographed by a hidden camera and having my picture displayed at the courtesy booth with the caption, "shopping cart pervert."

Time loses meaning in the silence of the supermarket. Within the windowless walls, there is no change of light or weather to distract me from my rounds. I can't tell if two hours have passed or 15 minutes. At the register, the cashier programs me for reentry into the outside world.

"How are you today?" she asks brightly. "Do you have our coupon card?"

"Fine. Yes," I answer in a groggy voice.

A moment later, I am blinking in the sunlight like someone recovering from a bout of narcolepsy. I sleepwalk to the car, dump the groceries in and drive away. A catchy tune comes on the radio and I sing along, finally released from the hypnotic silence. At home, my husband asks if I had a nice time shopping.

"I don't know," I answer. "I don't remember."

TOM, DICK AND LARRY BIRD

AY is atwitter. Everywhere you look the birds are making a ruckus, flapping about, calling on their ladies and making a general spectacle of themselves. If we acted that way we'd be arrested.

In the conservation lands, hardly a second goes by without a tweet-tweet or chirp-chirp from a bough or bush. It makes a person wonder, do individual birds have distinct voices the way we do? Birds of a feather sing the same song, but do some sound like Satchmo and others like Streisand—at least to each other?

Are there soprano finches and fat little chickadees with very deep chirps? Do baby birds only lurch around with open beaks when their mother speaks? Does Sarah the thrush know if it's Henry or Clarence calling from three trees over? Do birds ever stutter or ad lib, or speak with honeyed tongues like politicians? Are there unpopular birds with grating voices? Are they ever at a loss for notes?

Unfortunately, the only bird calls I can decipher are the ones in English. My favorite is "cheer-cheer" along with "bob-white," "quack quack" and "honk, honk." "Caw, caw" is the one that drives me to put a pillow over my head in the morning.

The others are difficult to remember. I have trouble with vowel-less sounds. There's a bird who squeals like a clothes-line being wheeled in but I have no idea of how to say or write the sound phonetically.

"Chit tchup," "kshlay kshee," and "tchack pruk" are songs described in my bird book but, strain as I will, I cannot distinguish them out in the field. The meadowlark sings "dzrrt" and the sparrow, "two extremely thin, grasshopper-like hisses," according to Peterson's Guide. I find it difficult to remember words I can't pronounce and can't recall a grasshopper's hiss offhand, so I remain unenlightened.

There is more we could know about birds. Do they nag each other? Are some birds smarter than others—lonely Einsteins on a telephone line? Do they have different personalities like puppies in a litter, with some more gregarious and others shy? Are some discreet and to be trusted not to utter a peep?

Do they look different to each other? Perhaps there are Rambo birds who strut and flex and Woody Allen birds who are short but funny. Are svelte birds admired more than stout; fluffy feathers more than flat? Are there wallflower birds who stay in their tree and others who are the life of the party? When you've seen one mourning dove, have you really seen them all?

I questioned my husband. "Do you think there are gifted birds? Birds that can belt it out like Ella or croon like Sinatra?"

He dragged his eyes away from his copy of Practical Sailor and peered at me over the page.

"It's a possibility," he said.

"You really think so?" I asked.

"Sure. Look out the window. Isn't that Ethel Merman hopping across the lawn with a worm in her mouth?"

LIFE AND DEATH BY FOOD

MY cousin, a successful city lawyer, called to inform me he read my column and liked it. I was quite pleased, him being so smart and all, until he said, "Do you want my critique?"

There was an icy silence. "Well," I said. "Yes. Of course. Sure, tell me. Go ahead and tell me."

"You write about food too much," he said.

"What do you mean? I certainly do not. I write about all kinds of things: birds, people and gardening and nature."

"Food. It's mostly food. You should deal with broader issues. There are millions of more important subjects to write about."

"Thanks for the tip," I said. Hmmmpf, I thought. He is probably one of those oddballs who orders from a menu instantly and doesn't care what he puts in his mouth.

It reminded me of a boyfriend I once had who said, "I eat to live, not live to eat." I should have known then that the relationship was doomed. He had no interest in food. He used to talk during meals.

I would sit across the table from him and watch his fork as he piled it with food, lifted it, as if to eat, then set it back on his plate. I was fascinated. He came so close to eating sometimes. It was if he was an actor on stage pretending to enjoy a meal. An hour later, his plate would be messy but full when the waitress came to clear the table.

I did what I could. I ate for the two of us and gained 20 pounds. Eventually, we broke up. I couldn't fit into any of my clothes and deep in my heart, I felt I couldn't trust him any more than someone who kicked the dog or hated babies.

I've been brought up to believe in life by food. All our important holidays are food holidays: ham or lamb on Easter, Christmas turkey or goose, Valentine's Day candy and hot dogs on the Fourth of July. It's unpatriotic to not care about food.

What's a birthday without a birthday cake, or a movie without popcorn? Beer and coffee are just beverages. Add pizza and doughnuts and you have a party. It's part of what makes us American.

I spend a lot of time thinking about what I am going to eat. In "Harry and Tonto," Art Carney indulges his cat and says, "Food is the highlight of his day." I agree. When I am not actually eating, I am planning what I am going to eat.

Should I have cereal for breakfast or a muffin? Perhaps I should skip breakfast altogether and have—ahh, a more substantial lunch? Will I be miserly today and live on a dole of fruit or will I splurge and wolf down pancakes like a lumberjack? I hoard my calories like a banker, trying to balance my deposits and withdrawals.

On occasion if I am depressed, I indulge in a mood called "Death by Candy." I do not drive from bridge to bridge and stare bleakly into the cold blue water. No. I march into my favorite candy store and buy chocolate covered almonds or truffles, or slip quietly into a drugstore for a jumbo bag of red licorice or a pound of baby Snickers. Revenge is sweet.

The nice thing about a candy suicide is I can repent the next day and sentence myself to a week of salad and poached fish.

My cousin doesn't understand how powerful food is. Seals and dogs and elephants and dolphins are trained with a food reward system. So are humans. It's a basic premise in our life. We go out to dinner to celebrate a raise or a promotion, a graduation or an anniversary. An award gets a reward.

So what's wrong with that? Now that I've written this, I am entitled to a handful of burnt sugar peanuts. If I didn't believe in the system, I'd never get any work done.

CLOSE THE DOOR ON CABIN FEVER

DOCTORS have recently come to the conclusion that cabin fever is a serious illness, rather than an imaginary complaint. Like the flu, it can spread quickly through an entire household or even a community. Doctors have reported that it has reached epidemic proportions this winter.

Age is no barrier; children, teens, adults and seniors are all at risk. Once contracted, the illness can linger for months.

Experts think the illness is caused by a combination of unrelenting gray days and extended periods of bitter cold weather that results in people staying indoors. Hence the term, "cabin fever."

Symptoms include irritability, boredom, restlessness, lethargy and hunger. Many patients complain that they are sick and tired of their home and the things in it, including small children and furniture. In extreme cases, spouses are included. Often people don't want to get out of bed in the morning.

Doctors have reported instances where people have strong urges to shave their head, lynch the dog, or move to Boca Raton. In one study, a couple who had been saving to buy a piano suddenly went into a music store and came home with a xylophone. Doctors have concluded that the illness has gone undetected for years.

Researchers have discovered that in some primitive societies, people believe that things get cabin fever too. The people in these cultures say that cars don't start, pipes freeze and furnaces get fussy. Skirts cling, doors warp, dust multiples and surfaces give off sparks.

Although pets cannot transmit the illness, they are known to be susceptible to it.

Symptoms can last up to four months and like malaria, can reoccur annually. Unfortunately aside from moving to a year-round warm climate, there is no known cure for the illness. But, like seasonal anxiety disorder (SAD), there are ways of coping with it.

The National Cabin Fever Research Foundation has the following suggestions, if you think you have experienced any of the above symptoms.

- Try going to a different post office, gas station and grocery store each week.
- Pretend you are living in another country. Iceland, for example. Buy a language dictionary and only speak Icelandic at home, even when the phone rings or the paper boy comes to the door.
- Buy and cook the native food of that country until spring.
- Price and tag all of your belongings for a yard sale. Compose an ad and set the date for April 1.
- Bake brownies and sell them door to door.
- Exchange your children with someone you know who has nice children. If it works out, consider making the arrangement permanent.
- Sleep at the opposite end of your bed.
- Offer to give someone else a home permanent.
- Move into a friend's house for a weekend, while they move into yours. Taking spouses and pets is optional.
- Try to get into the holiday spirit; address next year's Christmas cards now.
- Trade cars with someone for a month.
- Visit a pet shelter and walk a few dogs. Bring your own dog and let him know how lucky he is.
- Admit you hate all of your clothes; bring them to a friend's house and exchange wardrobes.
- Test drive the car of your dreams. Tell the salesman you just won the lottery.
- Eat nothing but cookies, candy and doughnuts for an entire day. Tell everyone you are a practicing vegetarian but just discovered you are allergic to vegetables.

- Look, at houses that are for sale in a neighborhood you admire, and find their flaws.
- Write an anonymous love letter to the most insufferable person you know.

WHAT TO GIVE THE QUEEN?

THE caption under the picture said, "President Bush admires a silver-plated horseshoe given to him by Queen Elizabeth II during an exchange of gifts at the White House."

I guess "admiring" is the euphemism the press uses when the president isn't smiling. He looked puzzled to me. As in, "Good grief, what am I supposed to do with this thing?"

Those lips that formed the words, "No new taxes," probably said, "Golly, your Highness, you shouldn't have. You won't believe this, but just the other day, I was saying to Barbara, 'Barbara, guess what I would die for? A matched pair of silver-plated horseshoes!' It's the truth. And now here they are. Is this a dream come true or what?"

I'm sure the president's brain was racing as soon as he unraveled the tissue. After all, the queen is only 65—not that old. She'll probably make another trip to Washington and expect those horseshoes to be on prominent display.

Given the situation, George did the best he could. He escorted the queen to the presidential pit. Yes, that is what they call it. And demonstrated how to pitch horseshoes before her very eyes. Not with the royal crested silver-plated horseshoes. No. He used his regular old, beat-up tarnished ones. The queen's spokesman said it was "certainly the first time she has seen a horseshoe thrown." Indeed. Very American.

Well, what do you expect? The president and the queen come from two distinct worlds and view things differently. We are talking the world's richest woman here. A woman accustomed to palaces, yachts, jewels, valets, ladies-in-waiting. A royal who travels around the world with six footmen, 20 tiaras, her own white kidskin toilet seat and an equerry (an officer in charge of the horses of a royal household).

George is out-doorsy but not part of the horsey set, although I'm not exactly sure what the horsey set does with silver horseshoes. George is a "Let's go fishing in Maine for the weekend" type. He gave her a fruit bowl.

George probably gives everybody fruit bowls. He strikes me as that kind of guy. I'm sure it was a nice one. A Bush family tradition. When in doubt, give a fruit bowl.

I can imagine the queen calling her son.

"Chuck, can you imagine getting a fruit bowl? Do they think we don't have one already? Thirty-nine years I've been queen, and they give me a present for a newlywed."

She was probably very gracious about it.

"Thunk you, Mr. President." The British are very courteous. I'll even bet she told her private secretary to make a note: "Serve George fruit, on his next trip to Buckingham. Wait. I've changed my mind. Hold it. Don't I still owe someone a wedding present?"

So what should George have given the Queen? She wanted to see a baseball game (so American); maybe he could have ordered a silver-plated baseball.

Or since she's into horses and gave him something horsey, the president could have given her a silver-plated fishing rod or something fishy. Trade silver hobby things.

This brings up the delicate question of whether you are supposed to give someone something *you like* or whether you should give them something *you think* they would like.

For instance, if George were thinking of himself, he could have given her a moosehead for her fireplace. Or if he wanted to tickle the royal sense of humor, a Bush-el of broccoli.

Or, if he were thinking of what the queen might appreciate, he might have given her Royal Dog-Bite Kit, since her Corgies are a bit snappish. Or, a red, white and blue kidskin toilet seat to commemorate the occasion.

The problem with all this higher-up gift giving is that the person can't return it and get what they really want. It's just too embarrassing to save the box or ask for the receipt. Can you imagine how mortifying it would be to get a credit at Macy's or the royal highness store and have the word get around?

The president will probably just pass those horseshoes along to the next visiting emir.

"Nice, George. Really nifty. I was just saying to my wives, 'Boy, could I use some new horsehoes!' What size are they?"

A TALE OF TWO SPORTSMEN

RUSTY, my neighbor's "Golden," and I were enjoying a late afternoon outing, he sniffing all the scents dogs love to sniff, and myself admiring the clear blue sky and russet marsh.

All the while, I had to stay alert because Rusty had been known to burrow into the tall grass and disappear into the Herring River for a quick swim.

We both saw the dark shape in the middle of the deserted road at the same time.

At first, I thought it might be a large turtle. When we got closer, we discovered it was a dead crow, not very big. It was lying on its left wing amongst the fallen leaves, with one yellow eye looking skyward. We stared at it, then, feeling a little spooked I urged the dog on.

Further down the dirt road, we passed empty shotgun shells: red plastic, 12-gauge, 3-inch magnum, No. 4 steel.

We ambled on, each absorbed in our own thoughts.

I couldn't get the image of the bird out of my mind. It was a fishing crow—a wary bird. I figured it had been hit by a car, but the more I thought about it, the more unlikely it seemed. No one could drive on an unpaved, pot-holed road that fast; besides, in the stillness of the marsh, you could hear a car coming a half-mile away.

Someone shot the crow.

On the way back, I stopped to look at it again.

The blue-black feathers gleamed in the sunlight; it was much prettier up close and I was not as nervous this time. I was mad.

Had a luckless hunter taken out his frustrations on this poor bird, then left the body on the side of the road?

The next morning, it was gone. Perhaps it had been a meal for some scavenger or, as I'd prefer to imagine, its fellow birds took it away. I walked briskly in the cool air, hardly aware of the occasional scurrying of chipmunks and rabbits. Suddenly, I heard a loud swish of wings overhead and turned to see a pair of snowy white swans flying low. My thoughts about the crow vanished in the pure beauty of the moment.

Approaching the footbridge, I saw a car pull up on the other side and a fisherman get out with a pole in hand.

We met on the bridge. I stood there admiring the autumn color scheme; he studied the surface of the water for signs of his evening's meal.

There was some rippling near the shore and he quickly rigged his pole.

"Looks like there's a fish caught in something down there," he said, and cast expertly to the spot. He was right, and managed to snag the line the fish was tangled in. He reeled in someone else's catch. Actually, it wasn't that easy. He had to climb down the bank and stumble into the cold October water to do it. When he was finished, he had pulled a two-or-three-pound striped bass from the river.

"This fish swam quite a distance. This is a deep-water lure he's caught in," he said respectfully.

The fisherman paused to untangle the heavy "No Alibi" trolling lure with a spinner and heavy wire leader attached, then gently lowered the fish back into the water and let it go.

As the bass swam away to be caught another day by another sportsman, the ripples settled into a fishless calm. The morning sun suddenly seemed warmer and the day ahead more promising as the dripping fisherman packed up his gear and headed home.

HIS, HERS: NOT JUST TOWELS

THERE are people who read poems from "The Prophet" at their wedding, or sing songs from the Bible: my husband and I recited excerpts from "The Territorial Imperative."

An invisible grid runs through our house, dividing our spaces into three zones: his, hers and neutral. We share the living room, dining room and common stairways. That is all. The rest of the house is carved out into territories.

The large two-story space known as "the future studio" belongs to my husband. Naturally, a big, yawning space such as that deserves to be infiltrated, particularly since it isn't functional yet.

"What's this stuff?" asks my husband. "Get it out of here!"

"They're Easter decorations," I calmly reply. "Where am I supposed to put them?"

"Who has Easter decorations?" he continues.

"We do. Remember the wonderful party we had in March?" I say, but he is taking an inventory of his flashlight collection.

"What's this?" I say, kicking at a pile of multicolored ropes.

"Lines for the boat," he answers, while testing all the batteries in all the flashlights.

"What are they doing all over the floor?" I've got him now; they don't belong in a future photography studio.

"I don't have any place to put them," he replies.

I don't give an inch. "Why don't you take them to the boat yard?"

"The boat isn't ready for them yet."

"So I'm supposed to vacuum around them for a couple of years till the boat's ready?" I ask rhetorically. I already know the answer.

This year, we had a his and her yard sale. We have his and her bookcases, his and her garden tools and his and her appliances. The food processor and compact disc player are his, even though I got them for Christmas.

I forged an office for myself in the basement; my husband built a workshop. He confiscated the garage; I invaded the guest bedroom.

He says, "You left your sewing machine in the studio."

I say, "Get your dinghy out of my office."

People say, "The house is so big."

I say, "Don't trip over the grids."

IT'S A RETRIEVER OF A HOUSE

DO you remember the red polo shirt you lost the last time you drove to P-town? The one that disappeared and you could never figure out how, because you didn't wear a towel home? Well, I have it and I'll give it back along with your missing Air Flow Nike with the plastic window in the sole. Your mismatched socks? I blush to admit I have the mates to those too. My home is a repository of the lost and misplaced. The home for little wanderers.

I find them under the car seat, in the dog's mouth and on the shelves of the garage. At the beginning of each summer I unearth a collection of unfamiliar beach towels that are as strange as the breakfast cereal in someone else's shopping cart.

"Did you put this here?" I ask my husband, pointing a finger at an important-looking bolt on the kitchen counter. "It wasn't there when I went to bed last night."

Scrutinizing it, he answers, "No."

"What's it belong to?" I ask, searching my appliances for an empty hole or loose appendage.

"Don't know, but it's very well made," he says reverently. "Better save it."

"I'm putting it here," I say, rejecting the responsibility for it. I tug open a drawer full of other oddities: keys that don't lock our doors or suitcases, peculiar gaskets, washers, screws and other gizmos that don't fit our toaster, blender or juicer.

The navy blue B.U. sweatshirt I wear when I'm painting or staining the house materialized out of nowhere about 10 years ago. I never bought it. No one gave it to me. And I didn't steal it. It's been around so long I've forgotten it isn't mine.

While some people may live in haunted houses, mine is a retriever. A magnet for drifting items.

I have a theory. Deep in the late hours of the night, the world tilts and objects from one kitchen roll into another.

Laundry driers fax socks to each other across the country. Shoes fly. Hubcaps wriggle off. Single earrings vanish. It is a nether world and my house is in the heavy traffic zone.

I'm thinking of starting a bureau of Unidentified Objects (BUO), but I can't seem to find my pen. *You* don't happen to have a green Schaeffer fountain pen, do you?

THE DIET PEPSI
GENERATION

WILL our children grow up with any sense of food nostalgia, now that they're wringing the calories out of food?

As a child, I was more like the family dog. Food was the high point of my day. My favorite question was, "What's for dinner?" I'd sniff around, not unlike the spaniel, trying to discover what was cooking on the stove or in the oven.

Sundays were agony, with pork or lamb roasting for hours. Just the thought of the quartered, crispy roasted potatoes that accompanied the meal makes me want to zip down to the super market and stock up. The fragrance of gingerbread, baked beans, chicken soup or corned beef and cabbage was ambrosia after a day of school.

I came from a family of foodies. My father was the King of Tantalizing Snacks. He'd carefully slice a left-over biscuit, lavishly cover it with thick pats of butter, then bury the whole business with strawberry jam. Cinnamon toast was performed, an evening bowl of cereal orchestrated.

"Umm," he'd say. "Want some?" Even though I wasn't hungry when he started, I was when he was through.

"Do you know what this would cost in a restaurant?" my father would ask when he came home with freshly caught fish, a deer in season or an occasional duck or pheasant. There was a reverence in our home for buttering toast so that no corners were missed, for choosing the smaller of the vegetables offered at a roadside stand and corn with little kernels. My mother spent more time picking our fresh berries, tomatoes and zucchini than she did choosing furniture for the house. Food wasn't merely for survival. It was a celebration, a reward for good grades, a festive holiday. It was love.

To me poor meant not having enough to eat. Rich meant bounty: a double-decker ice cream cone, a roast with leftovers, fudge loaded with walnuts. People weren't plump; they "looked prosperous."

Not so today. Rich is thin, fat is poor and chemicals are king. Real down-to-earth food, with calories created by God, is going the way of the dinosaur. No one gives a hoot about that old-fashioned word, moderation.

Who makes peach shortcake from scratch anymore, or cream puffs? People clap their hands in horror, not joy, at the prospect of a flaky home-made pie filled with dark chocolate pudding and crowned with tall peaks of real whipped cream. Food has become a sin. Something to be confessed: I thought fattening thoughts, I lusted after pictures in Gourmet Magazine, I envied someone's clam roll, I stole a Dove Bar from the freezer.

Our penance is to eat pharmaceutical food. We put "dextrose with dried corn syrup, aspartame, silicon dioxide, cellulose, tribasic calcium phosphate, and cellulose derivatives" (Equal) in our coffee along with "corn syrup solids, partially hydrogenated vegetable oil, sodium caseinate, mono- and diglycerides, dipotassium phosphate, artificial flavor and annatto (Coffee-mate) and call it breakfast. Our natural treasures have been replaced by fool's gold.

Children are growing up with guilt. Parents are stapling their stomachs and wiring their jaws to keep real food out. Weight control centers abound. Liquid diets and liposuction are popular. Food has become the enemy.

When I walk in the woods and smell wild blueberries ripening in the sun, a vision of my mother's pie wafts by me. I don't feel guilty. I feel sorry for the Diet Pepsi generation.

SHE'S NO LONGER SEEING RED

A MONTH ago, I was seeing red. It was always there, but I hadn't noticed. Then—POW. The color jumped out at me. It was everywhere. Little red cars, big red barns. Red lights, red sweaters, red stop signs, red hats, red packages. "Got to get me some of that red," I said to myself. The Christmas season does that to you.

So I bought red ribbon and holly and scattered it all over the house. I put bows on the candlesticks, decoys, stuffed teddies, plants, bannisters and wreaths. Now it's January and I can't wait to get rid of them. I hate red.

It is overbearing and tiresome. I am itching to pack away my red candles, napkins, tablecloths and ribbon. I cannot believe I will feel the same compulsive need for red next year, now that I've had my fix.

There was a time when I liked red. Even owned a red coat. Maybe that did it. Red is such an obligation—to be outgoing and cheery when some days you really feel more like puce or navy blue.

Today, my closet is full of neutral colors: beige, tan, brown and olive. In the red family, I prefer dusty rose. Maybe I'm mellowing or my taste is fading. Once, I refused to rent an apartment with red carpeting although it had a lovely view. A friend talked me into buying scatter rugs and I moved in. To this day, I have a clearer picture in my mind of the carpet than the view.

My husband says, "Red is the rarest color in nature." He has great respect for red. It should be used sparingly; a little goes a long way, like a red bow tie or a single rose.

I cannot imagine driving a red car or wearing red lipstick but red is quite popular. We are, after all, red-blooded Americans. Even Commies are Red (although not true to our red, white and blue). I admit to having a cat called "Big Red," although he is actually the color of marmalade.

"Red makes me think of Christmas and blood," says my mother-in-law. "Passion, fire, heat," says another friend. Personally, I don't know whether red is happy or cause for alarm. I think red is a little confused.

People turn red when they are embarrassed and see red when they are mad. Some businesses go in the red and others have red letter days.

The dictionary says a red letter (but not a Scarlet Letter) means "happy or memorable" and a red-letter day is "a fortunate, happy or auspicious day: so called because the holy days or saints' days were marked on the old calendars with red letters; a day of notable events or occurrences; a day to be remembered in a special manner."

On the other hand, there's a Red Dot Sale and the Red Light District.

Or painting the town red, which has nothing to do with paint, but means instead to "have a noisy good time, as by visiting bars, night clubs, etc."

You could be down to your last red cent or go one step further and actually be in the red. I'd much rather be in the pink.

Sailors beware of a "red sky in morning" and remember how to get home by chanting "Red, right, return."

The most famous red nose of all belonged to Rudolph. The second most famous belonged to W. C. Fields. And everyone knows the Red Cross, the Red Sox and Redd Foxx.

There are red necks, redskins and red herrings. The pestiest of squirrels is red. And it also makes a mean ant.

I'm glad it's January; my eyes need a rest from red. After the lush summer roses and the blazing plumage of fall, I need to fast on winter bleakness.

Today, I'll take down my Christmas decorations but maybe I won't pack away my red tablecloth. Valentine's Day is only a month away.

THEORIES
AND
THOUGHTS

FAT ATTACK

STAY off the streets if you know what's good for you. Thousands of pounds of fat cells have been released and are looking for a body to descend on. This Spring, our country is under a fat attack.

Most people are aware of Einstein's Theory, $E = MC^2$, or "Energy equals mass times the velocity of light squared." Translated into layman's terms, it means energy and matter are never lost, just transformed. You may not be familiar with the lesser known corollary of this theory which is: "When one person loses weight, another one gains it."

When fat is not on your body, it's invisible. It can take the unsuspecting by surprise. My friend Gail ate a tuna salad sandwich while relaxing on a park bench and gained a pound. She was sitting beside a young blonde in running shorts who was munching on a carrot stick. My neighbor Roland reported coming home feeling five pounds heavier after stopping to watch a road race. Now it's rumored in New York that Oprah's personal secretary can't squeeze into any of her old clothes.

No one discusses the fact that while teenage girls grow taller and thinner, their mothers get shorter and fatter. Some people complain that they gain weight without eating anything. Nobody gives them credence. Doctors point to the pituitary; colleagues secretly think they eat Twinkies in the supply closet; the victim thinks it's hereditary. No one realizes the consequence of carpooling with an anorexic.

This Spring, everyone is in a frenzy to get into shape. Parks and bicycle trails are sinking under the onslaught of joggers, walkers and speedo types. The air is thick with energy and it has to go somewhere. Haven't you ever wondered where?

Fortunately there is something you can do to prevent a fat attack. Stay indoors whenever possible. Drive alone. Don't linger in the produce section of your supermarket where aerobic junkies are fingering the grapefruit and rattling the melons. Beware of the low-calorie aisle, where Weight Watchers congregate, counting their food exchanges aloud like a mantra. Fat has to go somewhere. Stay out of its path.

Avoid people on liquid diets. The day will come when they will be put in quarantine; fat is bubbling off them like ginger ale. Do not lunch with salad eaters unless you want your matter changed. Visit with them on the telephone instead. If anyone you know is cutting calories, cut corners to escape them. Fat cells are indiscriminate. They will glomb on to anyone.

If you have begun to feel bulky or other people appear smaller to you, it may be too late. The best thing to do is associate with someone who is gaining weight. The formula also works in reverse.

TO NAP, OR NOT TO NAP

While I nodded, nearly napping,
suddenly there came a tapping,
As of someone gently rapping,
rapping at my chamber door.
  —*Edgar Allen Poe,*
  "The Raven," 1845

OH, yes, they've researched sleep. Some people don't need much; they can get along on three hours and still invent the light bulb while others need your good old eight hours. Sleep is basic, like bread and butter. What I want to know about is the jam. Naps, in other words.

Everybody knows someone who naps. In fact, all of us were big nappers when we were babies. And some countries like Spain and Mexico are famous for their naps or siesta, like the French are for their cooking. While all politics may be local, napping is universal.

So why isn't there more information available on the Common Nap? Why are they building tiny robots, the size of insects, that scurry around, bumping into each other over at MIT when their libraries must be full of dozing students? Wouldn't you think they'd investigate something a little closer to home? I mean, here we are, a nation of nappers and they're on their hands and knees making screwdriver adjustments to robots with bug brains.

Is napping good or bad for you? We'll probably never know, because our money is being spent digging up the remains of dead presidents. And look at that stamp incident. The Postal Service honored the late Hubert H. Humphrey, as well they should, with 300 million purple and white portraits of him on a 52-cent stamp. Unfortunately, the biographical researcher thought Humphrey became the vice president in 1964 instead of 1965, so all the stamps were printed with the wrong date. So of course they had to be destroyed, which cost you and me $580,000. "We didn't want to have a stamp out there with incorrect information," explained the Postal Service spokesperson. Looks as though someone was caught napping to me.

Not that I'm a regular nap taker. You don't have to do it yourself to be concerned. My mother-in-law schedules a little shut-eye every afternoon between 4 and 5. My husband never naps. But another friend can nod off at any time. And teenagers sleep so late, when they have the opportunity, it's like a night's sleep and nap combined.

I'd like to know if taking a nap is a sound investment. Is it one of life's bonuses? An extra? A perk? Or, dread of all dreads, is it a deduction from our Total Time on this earth? To be blunt, are nappers, in truth, sleeping their lives away?

A nap can be quite a pleasurable thing, particularly when accompanied by soft rain or a purring cat. But if this is time docked from our clock, we might want to be more circumspect about it.

Are our bodies like light bulbs with just so many hours of kilowatts in them? Are we wasting our incandescence in dreamland? Or is snoozing considered "downtime"? Are we merely recharging our battery? Should we feel virtuous or guilty when we're drowsy? Fight a yawn or give in gracefully?

Napping may even be worse than just wasting time, for all we know. Aerobic exercise is supposed to be good for us. Strengthens the heart and all that. Perhaps an anaerobic activity like napping does the opposite, weakens us, gives us low oxygen, low metabolism, that groggy feeling.

Where does the Surgeon General stand on napping? Should we be warned: Quitting Napping Now Greatly Improves Your Life's Expectancy. Should pillows state on the tag: Excessive Use of This Product May Be Harmful?

People could be dropping like flies due to nap addiction. Friends could be saying, "Poor guy, He was a heavy napper. Wouldn't listen to anyone. Took two a day; couldn't seem to kick the habit."

No one wants to admit it, but napping is pervasive. All across America it's happening in nursing homes and nurseries, in parked cars and on park benches. In bleachers and beaches, rocking chairs and recliners. In churches, concert halls, parlors and bedrooms. Every bus, train, boat and plane contains nappers.

Dogs nap, turtles nap, parakeets nap, politicians nap. Bodies in the arms of Morpheus. Napping occurs regardless of race, religion or creed.

I, myself, often think better lying down. My concentration improves when I close my eyes. My husband found me in this state, a little while ago.

"What are you doing? Napping!" he asked.

"No," I answered, without moving. "I'm doing research for a column."

THE ULTIMATE BAD HAIR DAY
OCCURRED A LONG TIME AGO

Only God, my dear,
Could love you for yourself alone
And not your yellow hair.

Yeats, 1865–1939

ONE day, a long, long time ago, man awoke and discovered he was bald. He ran his hands over his arms and legs. "Egad," he said. Actually, he wasn't completely bald, but then man is known to exaggerate.

His fur coat was gone, replaced by a more delicate coating of hair over most of his body. But he still had a luxuriant thatch on the top of his head. Could it be something I ate? he fretted. The woolly mammoth stew with the carrots al dente? Suddenly shamed, he hid his body under wildebeest skins, bison hides and a length of silk, tied with a square knot with sailboats on it.

Then, he worried that he would lose the only hair on his head he had left. He concocted a special soap and washed his hair gingerly. Then he trimmed it. And combed it this way and that. "I am definitely having a bad hair day. I hope I don't run into anyone I know," he grumbled as he prepared to go hunting. Then he paused. Maybe he should just stay home and plant vegetables. Tend to things around the cave.

Little did he know that the same thing was happening throughout the region. For several days, everyone stayed home. Then gradually, people ventured out to get the newspaper and buy a lottery ticket. When they encountered one another, they didn't point and titter. They said nothing.

But when they got home they studied their thatch of hair. Perhaps I should part it on the other side the way Barry does. Or, add a pat of bear grease like Reggie does.

The women did not adjust as easily. At first, they were loathe to trim what little hair they had. Instead, they rolled, pinned and curled it. They were inventive and copied things they saw in nature. They fashioned their hair into beehives, horse's tails and eventually, even cut it to look like their pet poodle's. But they were still dissatisfied. They wanted hair the color of honey and moonbeams or maybe a shade like Rhonda Flemming's.

The men thought they were nuts. A few decided to have a little fun and worked on potions they claimed would make hair shinier, stronger, cleaner and more manageable. The men laughed among themselves. It was a joke. But the women believed them. Soon the men who made the potions were making money but they didn't want to tell the women they were only kidding.

They whipped up concoctions from coconuts, apples and lemons that became all the rage. Of course, they made a few mistakes: one being the hair conditioner made from fish extract and ground periwinkle shells that caused house cats to sleep on their owner's heads.

But they worked the kinks out and pressed on. Mud, eggs, oil, bleach, dye. There was no end to what a person would put in her hair. Soon they were creating foams, sprays and gels. Women's hair started splitting and falling out. Scalps burned and peeled. Hair turned green. It didn't matter. The people were possessed with hair madness.

Insidiously, the word even crept into everyday conversations. Men proclaimed they wanted a "hair of the dog that bit them." Women sang, "I'm gonna wash that man right outa my hair." Gentle folk declared they wouldn't touch a hair on someone's head although their hair curled or stood on end when they were frightened.

Only one person saw how ridiculous it all was. But the women wouldn't listen to him and the men shunned him, saying he was a threat to free enterprise.

"One day, you will see the light," he said to no one in particular, since nobody paid any attention to him. "When man can fly like a pterodactyl on high and have pizza delivered to his door, he will recognize the truth." Alas, he died before his vision came true. The villagers grieved briefly, then forgot about him. Only his epitaph remains. "Hair today, gone tomorrow."

IS IT RIGHT TO
BE WRONG?

TWO shell fishermen tug quietly at their rig a few yards away. They are talking to each other, but I can't hear them even though my car window is down. It is Saturday and they are making the most of this mild winter day. Parked by the water, I am enjoying a presidential lunch—a junior cheeseburger deluxe; biggie fries and a coke. After a few ravenous bites, I relax. Now I can take my time and contemplate my surroundings.

I watch the fishermen, each in his own small boat. Neither wears a jacket; one is hatless. They rhythmically rake the cove. A study in efficient motion. My gaze drifts across the calm water to a pair of mergansers diving for their lunch. Their silhouette is cartoonish against the bright light. What funny ducks they are with their long pointy bills and wildly crested heads. They look plump yet angular in shape, like carved decoys.

The ducks almost lift themselves out of the water then plunge below to search for food. Disappearing beneath the surface, they then bob up in another location, five or six seconds later. A few buffleheads swim into view but the mergansers pay no heed.

I munch lazily on the french fries and watch all the industry before me. Feeling a twinge of guilt for having it so easy, I remind myself that I worked for my lunch too.

It is then that I notice a gull standing on the cracked pavement beside my car. He is staring at me with pale yellow eyes. When he has my full attention, he lurches forward, balancing himself with slightly extended wings.

A beggar gull. Well, I won't feed him. He should hunt for his own lunch and eat appropriate bird food the way the mergansers do.

I glance at him again and he moves a bit closer, cocking his head at me. His steps are wobbly. One leg is bent oddly. There is something wrong with him. Maybe a broken leg that didn't heal properly.

How can he hunt for food when there is something wrong with his leg? What do gulls eat anyway? The parking lot is strewn with broken clam shells—remnants of gull lunches. but what else do they eat?

Now he has my full attention. I notice he can fly when other birds threaten him. He just can't walk very well. Does a gull walk up to his lunch or fly to it? The bird looks old, if birds can look old. Tattered feathers. Dingy color. Not a sleek beautiful gull. Not worthy of a poem or story.

Drat. I toss him the crust from my burger. He limps over and gulps it down, looking up at me for more. I throw a french fry. And then another. With practice, my aim gets better and the gull doesn't have to hobble so far. Pretty soon, he can catch a fry in his beak. Then another gull spots the handout and lands nearby. The old gull and I wait for him to leave.

I wonder if I'm doing the right thing—violating natural order. If the old bird can't manage on his own, well, that's life. Only the strong are supposed to survive. It's population control. Instead, I am contributing to his dependency.

I toss another fry. My handout will get him through another day. The gull realizes I am out of fries before I do and disappears as suddenly as he came.

The fishermen continue raking shellfish in the silence. The mergansers have drifted farther away in search of food with the shy buffleheads in tow. Everyone is earning his keep.

I think about the gull. Maybe someone will park in this same lot tomorrow morning and toss him a piece of muffin. After all, theory is one thing, practice is another. When someone is hungry, how can you not share?

MAN CAME TO LOVE HIS LAWN

MY husband and I were out walking, when an intriguing question slipped from my lips. An important question, like others I've often asked: "What is the purpose of Life?"; "Why do people say, 'made from scratch'?" or "Do sheep get moth-eaten?" This morning's question was, "Who invented the lawn?"

Most properties have one—in varying shades of green or brown. But why? Is it an old fashioned custom or what? My husband warmed to the topic immediately and proceeded to concoct a theory based on goats, cows and sheep, who were, he announced, "The first lawnmower."

He has a way of turning every conversation into a discussion of tools. He went on to say that grass is everywhere. All over the world. One of the first, most primitive forms of life, coming right after lichen and gretchel.

Well, if this is true, how is it that all you see in gladiator movies is dust? Christians run from hungry lions and bang each other over the head with swords and there is nary a blade of grass in sight. The Romans didn't have lawns and without lawns they couldn't play golf and had to amuse themselves in other ways.

Oh, the Romans might have invented sandals so the dust would sift out of their shoes, but they didn't invent grasstrills so they could feel the grass beneath their feet.

Did they use electrolysis to pluck the blades of grass out or spread crushed hemlock around? Even if grass was frowned upon, wouldn't you at least see some in the slummy part of town? Think of how many Christians and lions we'd have today if they went to the Colosseum to watch football instead. It makes you realize we take lawns for granted.

Lawns are neat. They contribute oxygen, clean the bottom of our shoes, give children and adults a place to play, robins a location to hop and worms a roof over their head while they sleep.

A lawn is a sign of civilization. Entrances to caves might have had grass, but not a lawn. In 479 B.C., Confucious wrote, "The grass must bend when the wind blows across it." Nice, but not as profound as "The grass is always greener on the other side." That remark came later with lawns.

Shakespeare, Lord Tennyson and Walt Whitman wrote about grass, as did our contemporaries Allen Ginsburg and Timothy Leary, but I think they were thinking of a different type.

The transformation of grass to lawn symbolizes the evolution of man from hunter to herder. Then a housewife took the next giant step forward for mankind. She got fed up with the first animal lawnmower.

"This place is a zoo. I don't want those cows and geese all over the front yard. And take off your smelly shoes before you come in the house. Can't you watch where you walk?"

So her husband dutifully built a fence to contain all the animals. To their surprise, the grass grew as high as a dinosaur's ear. "Cripes, I hope I don't drop my car keys out there," said the husband.

"There are bugs in the grass, the size of yo-yos" said the wife. "Cut it."

"You cut it," he answered. "I'll do the pots and pans." She wouldn't trade and he developed a severe case of lawn knee that summer. But the neighbors came by and admired his work.

"What do you call it?" they asked.

"A lawn," he answered. A new era was born. Pretty soon, personages of great status and enlightenment were called "Your lawnship," which roughly translated to, "He who is wise and keeps the bugs from the door." Later, through a lot of misspelling, the term deteriorated to "Your lordship."

The mechanical lawnmower took man out of the dark ages and transported him to a world of new delights: baseball, golf, soccer, egg rolling and pink flamingos. It even instilled in him a sense of territory. Never again did he wish he was inside, doing the pots and pans.

MELTDOWN TO INVISIBLE

THE '80s and the Era of Conspicuous Consumption are over but now something more insidious is developing: The Age of Invisible Consumption.

An acquaintance tells me he bought an "Infiniti," sight unseen and loves it. No one I know has actually laid eyes on the vehicle yet, but he goes around acting serene and jiggling car keys in his pocket and muttering things like, "The rustling leaves become one with the inner sound of nature."

Something is happening here and it is just the tip of the iceberg. The advertisements for invisible fencing never show a picture so how can you tell when the people who install it are through? Does anyone who has one know if it works?

The newest thing is invisible makeup. Max Factor has come out with a mascara that promises, "No more raccoon eyes." "Ring around the collar" wasn't enough of a guilt trip; now we're threatened with ring around the eyeball. There is finally a product that looks like nothing when you put it on and cost the same as the real thing. No one will buy it, you say? Wrong. They sold six months of stock in one week. You can imagine how excited the cosmetic industry was; they gave Max Factor their top award and Forbes listed the product as one of the 10 hottest of the year.

If we had been paying attention, we could have seen this trend coming. Remember how large everything used to be? Radios and television sets were the size of sofas. Big was better. "Eat, eat," our mothers used to say. Well, that's all over.

Now everything is smaller: calculators, magazines, computers, and candy bars. Someone uttered the words, "Tiny is terrific," and people rushed to buy miniature poodles, bite-sized Shredded Wheat, microchips, compact cars, pygmy ponies, dwarf vegetables and complicated electronic equipment the size of an eraser.

Everything from soup to news is condensed. When is the last time someone asked you to enlarge on a subject?

Husbands, wives, children, bosses and lawyers all say, "Get to the point."

To make a long story short, flesh is out, bones are in.

It's reached epidemic proportions. Buses and vans have gone mini. "Honey I Shrunk the Kids" has been released on video. Houses are chopped into condos. Television programs are full of fast pans and quick bites. Less has become more and we are headed toward nothingness.

My biggest fear is that they'll come up with invisible food. I wonder if the restaurants will bother to wash the dishes after they serve it. Any day now, a big company will come out with the perfect product that all of America is waiting for and advertise the daylights out of it.

It will have no sugar, no salt, no fat, no carbohydrates, no cholesterol and no protein. It will be free of chemicals, additives, preservatives and dyes and at the same time All Natural and Lite. When you open the package, there'll be nothing inside. I could be enthusiastic if I could pay for it with invisible money.

A CASE OF SELECTIVE MEMORY

MY husband is fond of saying the cat has a brain the size of half-a-walnut. He does this to aggravate me. I think the cat is smart. Now I'm beginning to think my own brain has shriveled to the size of a raisin.

When a station attendant gives me directions that have more than two turns, I have to stop at the next station for a recap. Then, I turn to the passenger riding with me and ask, "Did you get that?"

"You know the dress I wore to the wedding last week," asks a good friend, "Do you think it would be okay for the Smothers' anniversary party?"

"Ummmm." I answer. I don't even remember what *I* wore.

"How long does the exterminator take? asks a neighbor with a flea problem.

"Don't know," I answer.

"Didn't they come to your house?"

"Yes, but I don't remember."

My brain can only hold about four phone numbers before it gets overtaxed and confused. If I learn a new number, I lose an old one. The same is true of ZIP codes. I'm so sure I'll remember the ZIP of a place I've lived, I don't write it down in my address book, then when I want to send Christmas cards to former neighbors, I sit around mumbling "02, 02 02-what?" How could I forget? Easy. I moved to the Cape and my memory space was taken up with new numbers. My brain is like a small house. There's not enough room for a lot of furniture.

For years at dinner parties, loftier brows than mine have discussed the merits of Hamlet and Macbeth while I mutely scraped the crumbs off my dessert plate. I felt educationally deprived until I ran across a copy of my college transcript. I had a semester of Shakespeare. Not only had I forgotten the plays, the words and the characters, I had even forgotten I had taken the course.

Actually, I have an impressive list of things I've forgotten. I went to photography school, but forgot how to process film. I learned how to SCUBA dive and passed my PADI certification, but I don't remember what an atmosphere is or how to check out a dive buddy. I scored in the 90s in a safe boating course, but have forgotten my navigation and knots.

Every now and then, I try to remember whether the Earth goes around the sun or the moon goes around the Earth or the sun goes around everything, even though it was explained to me in an unforgettable fashion with a flashlight, grapefruit and orange.

I don't mean to imply that I am blithering. Some things stand out in sharp relief: I remember every flat tire and permanent I've ever had; the pie crust I made with two to three cups of shortening instead of 2/3s of a cup; the opening scene of "My Fair Lady," the first play I ever saw, and any oral history that begins with "Remember the time..."

When my husband says, "But I told you yesterday," my mind is a blank. I don't mind. I used to think he had an excellent memory, but his is just as bad as mine. He doesn't remember what I tell him, either.

Actually, I don't think my memory bank is failing. It's just that it's like the savings and loan institutions; as time goes on it gets more selective about what it invests in.

THE LAMENT OF THE TONGUE

WORK, work, work, that's all the tongue ever does. When it's not helping us converse, it's assisting us with a mouthful of Egg Foo Yong. Sure, it could be worse. We could be washing ourselves like a cat or licking our wounds like a dog. But the fact is, the tongue is much too busy already.

Hardly a day goes by when it doesn't go to bed exhausted. Sometimes with Oreo crumbs still stuck to it. The tongue is a droll little fellow who enjoys his job and courteously waits until morning to remind you to brush your teeth.

The tongue is primarily known as an organ of speech. You'd think one function would be enough. It's a full-time career, shaping and articulating words. But no, our tongue is a workaholic.

A bit of a snoop, it perceives food, checks out the taste sensation, then—if it's a go—helps us ingest our food. A tidy devil, the tongue also pitches in to keep up the grounds around it; operating as a windshield wiper after you eat a jelly donut and a homing device if you get a piece of lobster stuck between your teeth.

Some consider the tongue too low brow. Too muscular, they say. All brawn and no brains. But its reflexes are good. Startled, it will deliver a scream first and ask questions later.

A tongue doesn't mind criticism, however. It's very good-natured. A down-to-earth organ. Not the least bit temperamental. It doesn't need bells, sirens or fireworks to keep it operational. Unlike the heart, which is constantly breaking and mending or sending ominous signals for attention.

The tongue never acts uppity. It doesn't claim to be the throne of the soul or the seat of the imagination. The tongue has its feet on the ground. It craves no enhancement: no ribbons, jewels or tattoos. A perfect servant, the tongue. Unlike the complainer of all complainers: the stomach—"I'm hungry," "I'm too full," "That was too spicy," "Where are my Tums?"

The eye is arrogant compared to the tongue. Pretentious, it thinks itself the connoisseur. But which can discern the difference between salt and sugar, a ripe melon or bland, if chocolate is bitter or bittersweet?

The tongue accepts its lot in life. Out of sight, out of mind. It has but one motto: "Don't bite the tongue that feeds you." Tongues are not snivelers. They don't drip, ache, break, pound or fall asleep at the wheel. They develop no corns or calluses regardless of use.

Best of all, they seldom wear out or have to be transplanted. Instead of taking an early retirement like the ears, eyes and teeth, the tongue hangs in there, plugging away for all its worth. It's about the only organ you can count on until the very end.

Does it get any appreciation for this devoted service? No. There are no great legends about the tongue, no juicy parts in the theater, no memorable lyrics, no famous paintings.

Oh, a few people have made up tongue sayings. Publius Syrus made an astute observation in the 1st century B.C.

"Let a fool hold his tongue and he will pass for a sage."

And mothers have always said, "Bite your tongue," or "Can't you find your tongue?" Sometimes people had the words "on the tip of their tongue." Tales were told "tongue in cheek," religious fanatics spoke "in tongues" and the hungry stood with their "tongue hanging out." Liars had "forked tongues," gossips had "wagging tongues." Those who weren't "tongue-tied" might amuse others with a "tongue-twister" or send them running with a "tongue-lashing."

There are "native tongues" and "foreign tongues." Now the only time you hear about a tongue is when the doctor asks you to stick it out.

The tongue has been lost in the shuffle of the modern world. If it could, the tongue would remain a toddler forever, catching snowflakes in midair, making funny faces, licking lollipops and cool windowpanes—innocent of the difference between ice cream cones and stones, walls and dolls, spoons and rooms, candy and whatever else is handy.

Ah, the poor tongue, the only thing it can't do is speak for itself.

RICH OR POOR, WE CAN'T FORGET OUR DEBTS

GLANCING over the Sunday paper, I comment to my husband, "At least you're not $115 million in debt, like Donald Trump. And that's down from $975 million," I add.

He laughs. But all those zeros make me dizzy. I cannot imagine how anyone can owe that much money. Even The Donald, who got married again at 46 and started a second family.

If this man won the biggest lottery on the planet, he'd still be in debt—albeit, a fancy sort of debt, where he still gets to live in a 25-room Trump Tower apartment, wear elegant custom-made suits and have the barber come to him.

I study the newspaper picture. He is wearing a crisp white shirt, red power tie and a smirk. The Donald, I decide, will spend the rest of his life clawing his way to the top of money mountain. When he pays off his debt, he will try to recoup the fortune he had before. And then better it. He will never have enough money.

Meanwhile, his life won't visibly change. Unless he adds on a 26th room to his apartment. Or finds a third wife. It's hard to understand a guy like him. He doesn't need dollars. He needs sense.

Most of us do share something in common with The Donald, however: the desire to pay off all of our bills and live debt-free. And have a little left over for security. "Enough to last," as one elderly woman I know put it. It's just a matter of degree. Meanwhile, our life goes on just like The Donald's. Well, not quite like The Donald's.

Deep down, in our buy-now, pay-later hearts, owing money makes us nervous. After all, as the bard said, "Neither a borrower nor lender be." But we didn't listen. Particularly since Visa is much nicer to do business with than a loan shark.

That's why lotteries are popular. They provide that one person in a trillion a chance to get out from under, and more. It's the more part that's scary.

Maybe Christopher Ramesar of Albany is just as well off without the $10 million New York Lotto pot he sort of won but didn't. Mr. Ramesar mailed in $150 for 26 weekly drawings on May 7. The numbers he chose were drawn on July 17. The problem was his application wasn't processed until four days after the drawing. So he didn't get the $10 million. He probably would have been happier if he hadn't played at all.

Most of us would be content with a mere half-million. Enough for a decent house, a good car and premium toilet paper. But not enough to set the phone ringing, screw up the day job or our sense of self worth.

Recently, I read a book about a woman who wins a $60 million lottery. She immediately goes out and buys a couple of cars, lots of expensive clothes, a million-dollar mansion; hires a staff of gardeners, maids, and cooks; then takes a cruise. She made me nervous. I was afraid she was going to run out of money before the end of the first chapter.

As a millionaire, she has plenty of problems. But they get resolved as they always do in novels. Most of us will never find out how we would handle sudden wealth, if that swing of the pendulum would bring us joy or misery. So we keep plugging away, trying to get rid of our debts. Just like The Donald.

ENGLISH HAS BECOME THE DAGWOOD OF LANGUAGES

"The difference between the right word and the almost right word is the difference between lightning and the lightning bug."

— *Mark Twain*

SOMETIMES you think you know someone really well, like your husband or best friend, then out of nowhere, they start speaking a language you have never heard before. Words you didn't know existed.

"The knuckle thickness should correspond with the flange width so it can close over the front of the carcase," says my husband to the carpenter, to let him know that he is no ignoramus and he'd better not pad the bill.

Mention anything to do with water: sea, ocean, lake, wet—and he bursts into Boatese. "A dodger coaming, for the attachment of the bottom forward edge of the dodger, makes installation easier and creates a better water seal," he'll say, thoughtfully.

"Ummm," say the landlubbers, "How are the kids?" But it is too late. Any sailor within hearing range, will chime in, "Right. And, the heel of the mast should be bolted to the step or pinned through the tabernacle."

I head for the onion dip with visions of the Tabernacle Choir performing on our deck. I do not speak sub-languages. Oh, some of them I can decode. Like Michael Keaton saying, "Do you want the tin?" in "One Good Cop." Or the kids mumbling, "We're talking dial tone here," when they want to put down someone's intelligence. Then there's the "Wuv you, tweety-poo," language of love.

But I do not understand my doctor when he says, "We must lower the level of and treat the complications of atherosclerosis by a modified diet. In other words, the hypercholesterolemia equals the serum cholesterol. Now do you have any questions? No? Good."

Golfers discuss birdies that aren't in the trees; birders describe Gaviiformes, Podicipediformes and Procellariiformes. A cavity can be invisible or as big as a cave, depending on who is doing the talking—your doctor or dentist.

"In the can," may mean a movie has been completed, a criminal has been put away, or someone can't come to the phone right now. It's a wonder we learn to communicate at all.

"Menkalien is a spectroscopic binary and the double star at 2984 is actually multiple, part of a cluster," is not an opening for the question, "What's your sign?" Astrology and astronomy just sound like sisters.

A scaly rhizome is not an animal that predates the dinosaurs. It is a member of the Gesneria family. The Gesneria family is related to African violets, not Bugsy Siegel.

Portfolios can be multicolored or all green depending on whether you're an artist or investment broker. Icons appear in churches and on computer screens. There's no such thing as plain English. Our language is a sandwich whose name is Dagwood.

"Bosomy southern lusciousness" is not a line out of Faulkner but a description from "The World Atlas of Wine." What has happened to our manner of speaking?

There's dog breeder talk, lawyer Latin, and auto mechanic gibberish. We're surrounded by financial phraseology, advertising lingo, real estate vernacular and insurance idiom. It's as if everyone is speaking in tongues.

There must be secret societies, who meet like the Kiwanis Club on the first Wednesday of every month, and make up new words and meanings, while the rest of us go around saying thingamabob, gizmo and doohickey.

No wonder I haven't mastered a foreign language. I haven't learned English yet.

GROWING UP, GROWING OLDER

I'VE spent 40 years growing up and almost a decade growing older.

The transition still comes as a surprise to me. Sometimes, it's physical, like when I pant up the stairs with my groceries or creak down into a squat position at my post office box.

Other times, it's financial—like shelling out $6 for a movie or $7 to have a linen dress pressed. I'm in a price warp. Mentally, I'm back in the '60s, humming "Golden Oldies" instead of steaming ahead toward the '90s.

My mirror doesn't lie, but I do. I see wrinkles, strands of gray and a lower center of gravity, but somehow, I edit them out so that the reflection that flosses its teeth with me is younger—the way I remember myself.

Only in snapshots or family videos do I see myself as others do. Still, I dismiss the image, blaming the camera or unflattering angles—it must be exaggeration, like a distorted recording of my voice. (Do I really sound like that?)

No, the changes I see are in the outside world; in the fresh young faces concentrating on the computer screen at the bank, or the beardless policemen waving traffic by, or the fledgling doctors riding the hospital elevators.

Somewhere in time, my perceptions have changed. I mistake 25-year-olds for teenagers, and older people don't look so old anymore.

Somehow, I've been shifted up a rung or two on the staircase of life. A new generation has taken over my former foothold.

The notion that "Being around young people keeps you young," is nonsense. If they weren't around, I probably wouldn't realize I was older.

The first time I detected I was inching toward my dotage, I was shopping in a produce store and had asked a clerk to weigh some fruit.

"Here you go, ma'am," he said, handing me my grapes.

"Ma'am?" I thought to myself. "Not Miss?" While I was chewing over his choice of words, I realized *I was older;* otherwise, I wouldn't have had the nerve to ask him to wait on me.

My friends have been beached on the sands of middle age with me, but not the rest of America. New models, athletes, and TV personalities have replaced our generation of role models. We are not the same age as the rest of the world anymore.

I have started counting down the years I have left. I am spurred on by the obituary page. I check the age and cause of death of total strangers with a certain fascination and am reassured by those who die peacefully at 91 or 102.

An untimely death has the opposite effect; I feel lonely and frightened. Melancholy. A line from John Donne plays in my mind:

". . . any man's death diminishes me, because I am involved in mankind; and therefore never send to know for whom the bell tolls; it tolls for thee."

Occasionally, I recognize the name of a former teacher or the parent of an acquaintance; sometime it's a contemporary. Death has become more familiar.

This week, my husband and I both lost a family member. With my uncle's death, I realize my father's generation is gone. It is strange to realize that I am the age I remember my parents being, and now sound and talk like them when I speak to the young. I have moved up the ladder.

To me, growing older used to be a wish list. It meant maturity and grace, having the right answers, control at my fingertips, and wearing a sparkling mantle of wisdom. I never anticipated the surprises.

OFF THE
BEATEN
TRACK

THE NOSE KNOWS BEST

I THINK the nose is under-rated. Everybody writes about eyes and mouths, how one is the window to the soul, and the other, the way to the heart. Well, big deal. They're not as noble as the nose.

The eye is unreliable. They say people eat with their eyes, but no one mentions the indigestion you get from optical illusions. Open a mouth and you find overrated taste buds. That's why cola companies have those taste tests all over the place. They've got a 50-50 chance of you choosing the right one, better odds than Las Vegas. It's like batting .500 already. You can't blindfold the nose. It is infinitely more clever than taste buds. It knows.

In literary circles, taste gets all the press. Oh, there's, "Keep your nose to the grindstone," or "Plain as a nose on a man's face," and "He has a nose for news," and "Paying through the nose," but nothing that does it justice.

Cyrano de Bergerac said, "A great nose indicates a great man," but no one took him seriously; they thought he was blowing his own horn. There are few celebrity noses: Jimmy Durante, Bob Hope, Pinochio. Other countries and cultures relish the nose, however. They paint it, stud it, ring it and decorate it with whalebone and bright beads. Eskimos kiss with it.

Sadly, we are out of touch with our nose. Oh, we give it attention when we have colds and dab sun block on it to keep it from peeling, but olfactory sensations like delicate nosegays and rousing smelling salts have gone the way of the Palmer Method. It's not fair.

The nose never complains. Babies use their noses as bumpers in their formative years and elders wear their bifocals on them. Unlike eyes and teeth, the nose's upkeep is minimal. It performs an aesthetic service as well, by aligning the face and giving it symmetry. We have two eyebrows, two eyes, two ears—the piece de resistance is the nose. It's like a sofa pulling a room together. Without it, we'd look pretty boring.

The nose is not fickle. It doesn't say, "Yes, yes," when it means, "No, no." There are no bedroom noses. Some people use their nose to sneer or silently voice disdain; unfortunately, there is nose abuse.

You can follow your heart or you can follow your nose. Your nose can tell you it's going to rain, your house is on fire or it's time to clean out the refrigerator. Most hearts can't find their way out of a paper bag.

Noses are happy around freshly cut grass, cook-outs, leather car seats, lilies of the valley, warm bread and clean sheets. They cannot be deceived by silk flowers or stuffed animals.

Noses are known for their excellent memories. One visit to a dentist's office and they remember it forever. They are more multi-lingual than the brain and recognize Italian, Chinese and French cooking when they smell it.

They are also astute. They know the difference between the cut wood odor of a new home and the milky clean scent of a new baby. They can differentiate between lilacs and daisies, cantaloupe and strawberries and mildew and morning dew. It's a wonder they aren't on the Organ Donor List.

Like bears, noses tend to hibernate during the winter. They perk up around wet mittens and chimney smoke but it usually takes the fresh green scent of spring to bring them around. Summer with its rich extravagant perfumes is their favorite season.

Most noses adore Cape Cod—the fragrance of salt, brine and sun, the fog mixed with pine, even the clammy smell of low tide. They'd rather be here than anywhere. They're smart, these noses.

TRAINING TODDLERS
FOR SPACE

WHILE we're trying to unravel the complexities of our own life, like locating our warm socks for these cool mornings and determining whether it is cheaper to mail a check to the bank or drive there, the folks at NASA are dealing with more urgent matters. They are pretending to grow potatoes in outer space.

A presidential panel has proposed to send Americans to Mars around the year 2014 and NASA is preparing for it. That's only 18 years from now. Our future astronauts are probably playing in a sandbox or having a nappy-nappy at this very moment.

Little do they know, that in addition to having "The Right Stuff," they will have to learn gardening. Not the way you and I do, digging around in the muck battling rabbits, pulling weeds and hitting ourselves on the head instead of bugs. No. These little guys, who are still in their "Oshgosh" overalls, will be working in soil-less gardens.

And they won't need green thumbs because they'll be tending a computer garden. This doesn't mean they will be harvesting electrodes and nodules. They'll be growing real food

So far, NASA has developed dwarf wheat, lettuce, soybeans and the above mentioned potato. Coming soon are sweet potatoes, string beans, carrots, peanuts, tomatoes, radishes and maybe rice.

I think NASA would do well to keep this list to themselves, at least until the kiddos are a little older and realize that Oreo cookies do not grow on trees and peppermint ice cream is not a crop.

Anyway, these computers will control everything the hydroponic plants need, like water, light, heat and mineral replenishment. The astronauts will view the progress on a television screen. Yo. The kids will like that. Although, let's face it, how compelling can it be to watch soybeans grow?

Paul Buchanan, head of biomedical operations and research at the Kennedy Space Center, described the job to the Associated Press. "You will do some chemical analysis of the nutrients. You will make absolutely certain that the nutrient revitalization system is working as it should. You will monitor the air inflow and outflow. You will monitor the character of the condensate."

Yawn. I think they had better concentrate on the space travel part.

It will take a year to travel to Mars, another year to get a feel for the place, check it out, write postcards and take pictures, then another year to get home again. That's why the astronauts will have to grow their own food. Shrewdly, NASA realizes grocery deliveries in outer space might pose problems. And be expensive.

I am glad they thought of this. Imagine waiting a year for a Domino's Pizza and it finally arrives, you tip the delivery kid a half-a-trillion, then open the box and there's this slithery, furry thing in there that growls when you try to slice it.

Besides, supply ships could get lost or hijacked by whatever is lurking around hungry in the galaxies. It definitely makes sense to bring your own garden with you. Why take chances? That's why I have a suggestion.

I think they should isolate the most promising astronauts now and protect their taste buds from Big Mac attacks. I mean, what normal, red-blooded American kid has ever had an uncontrollable urge for dwarf wheat and string beans? Or radishes? In other words, maybe we should grow children to go with the vegetables.

We've got to train these little guys while they're young. Neatness is a trait that should be learned. On a space ship, everything has its own special place. Like a toybox. All the knives and forks have their niches, there's a special drawer for your space pajamas, a slot for your toothbrush, the toilet paper has to go in the toilet paper holder. Otherwise, the stuff would be floating around all over the place. A mess. Like living in a laundry dryer.

You have to pack properly. Economy is important. There's not a lot of space when you're in outer space. Forget knick-knacks, stuffed teddy bears or the odd pot with no top. Everything must be functional, usable, and reusable.

"For any kind of extensive manned exploration or habitation in space . . . you're going to have to recycle," says Paul Buchanan. And there will be no littering in outer space. No rolling down the window and dumping an empty beer can or unloading an old sofa under the cover of a dark planet. Already, they're able to recycle water, oxygen and inedible plant parts (by breaking them down with friendly fungi and bacteria).

Their next goal is to recycle human waste. As plant nutrients. This cutting edge of recycling is due to begin next year, giving the "You are what you eat" proponents lots of time to digest the idea. Do you know someone in diapers you could recommend for the program?

NOT ALL IS GILDED
FIRE HYDRANTS

"**W**HAT shall we write about this week?" I ask the cat. He is lazing about on my desk beside the typewriter with the empty sheet of paper in it. He blinks but doesn't answer. We go through this every week.

By now people will be wandering through the house with mangled shreds of wrapping paper stuck to their feet, wondering how they're going to pay their January bills. The day after Christmas is always gloomy, I tell him. Maybe we should detach. Write about junk in space. Or how to tell if your neighbor is a space alien: how they talk to themselves to practice our language; eat the box rather than the cornflakes; have mood changes when the microwave is on; don't understand the concept of matching socks..."

The cat yawns. Maybe if there were alien mice or space bugs.

I drum on the keys of my typewriter.

"Well, how about the guys who predict what will happen in the stock market from astrological observations. They're supposed to be 80 to 90 percent accurate. They call them—business horoscopes."

The cat looks down at his paw and starts to delicately wash it.

"Look I didn't make it up! Texaco and Coca-Cola are Virgos and 1997 is supposed to be a very good year for them."

The cat is washing his ears with his paw.

"These guys call themselves astro-economists and they study the gravitational forces of Venus and Jupiter and stuff and the Earth's tidal flows and weather patterns and the rise of the moon. . ."

The cat is definitely not paying attention. I tap a pencil on his head.

"Did you know that most women and apes cradle their babies in their left arm? No, you didn't know that, did you? Well, it's because they think emotional information is handled by the right side of the brain which is directly fed by the left ear and the left side of the visual field. If a mother holds her baby on the left side, she keeps her right brain free to respond to . . . Are you listening to me?"

The cat has dozed off.

I reach for the orange box of Iams and rattle it.

"Bet this will interest you. Why can't President Bush catch fish?"

Aha. The cat is staring at me.

"No tasty trout. No succulent striped bass. No delectable bluefish for that good doggie, Millie."

The cat's tail flicks slightly at the mention of the White House Dog, then his eyes begin to close, so I rattle the box of cat food again.

"Millie's life isn't all gilded fire hydrants and walks in the Rose Garden. Millie's daddy can't catch fish and it's not because he's a lousy fisherman. No, it's because. . ."

The cat's eyes are wide. He is finally paying attention.

". . . He repulses fish. That's right. Fish don't like the way our President smells. He secretes an amino acid called L-serine, according to a Dr. Gregory Bambenek, who tested a fingerprint Bush left at a 1988 fishing tackle show in Springfield, Missouri. He claims fish loathe and fear the scent of L-serine, which is secreted by sea lions, bears and some people like President Bush. Professional bass fisherman secrete very little of it. Bush tested a 12 on his chart.

"So when Bush baits his hook, he gets this L-serine all over it and the fish swim in the opposite direction. They have very good noses. Fish can detect repellent substances at a dilution of one part per 80 billion."

The cat gets up to stretch. I speed up my delivery.

"But there's good news! The President can buy a bottle of Dr. Juice Hand and Lure Cleaner or Dr. Juice Chewee Juice Scent, which is composed of impregnated biodegradable crickets, mayflies, minnows and crawfish. Then he'll be able to catch fish for poor Millie."

The cat leaps off my desk and saunters down to the kitchen. All this fish talk has made him hungry. I follow. Maybe a little snack will give us some inspiration.

REFLECTIONS OF A
CAVE BEAR

IT'S two days after Christmas and all through the house, the only thing that's being stirred is the Alka Seltzer. Even the mice are pooped. Nestled amongst dry pine needles and shreds of wrapping paper are a left glove and a right slipper. The rest of the trophies from under the tree have found their way into closets and drawers.

The lights are still twinkling every nanosecond, but my accompanying eye twitch has finally disappeared. The cat yawns at the ornaments and has stopped throwing up tinsel. Cookies with brightly-colored sugar have ceased moving, even with a bribe of hot chocolate.

I am almost over the turkey massacre which occurred when He Who Does Not Belong in the Kitchen turned the bird from its back to its tummy, ripping off both legs and the attached meat in the process. The skeletal remains were served up on a platter looking like something that was hit by a car.

Unwritten Christmas cards sit waiting to be packed up with my good intentions for next year. The high hysteria is over. It is time to act ordinary again.

Now I can go back to concentrating on serious matters like keeping the birdfeeder full and not running out of mayonnaise. Four days to New Year's, then the festival of lights will be over. The season of expectations will dissolve like a melted snowflake. We'll be free of the cardinal rule of the holidays: "Thou shalt be merry." We'll be able to go about our grumpy way without feeling guilty or out of sync.

The winter doldrums will begin. Out with the red and green (except in Gucci-dom) and in with tonal shades of gray. It's time to settle into scratchy wools and bleak landscapes and review the past. Tally up our successes and mistakes. Remember those who won't be ringing in the New Year.

The first day of the first month is coming and our numbering system takes us back to "go." We have a chance to begin again.

I like looking behind me and ahead; it's my measure of the present. Winter is an enforcer. It traps me indoors like a cave bear, forcing me to rest and reflect. And plan.

Leisurely I try to map out the next season of my life as if it were a garden, choosing what I wish to plant, nourish and watch grow. Do I want to take more chances or fewer? Reach out for more or restrict myself to less?

It's a time to get to know myself in a bare-bones way. I'm like an empty garden. The year ahead is full of choices, but there's lots of time to savor them, learn from gardens past. What was too ambitious and failed? What was too easy and unchallenging? What got out of control? What was neglected? What gave pleasure or caused pain?

I have time to unravel what I really want from what I think I want. Blissfully, the ground is frozen so I can't make any quick decisions. I must wait. It's the season to reflect early and often. It's the season for thought.

THE BUNGLER'S COOKBOOK

BROWSING through a bookstore, trying to pass the time away until spring arrives, I picked up a cookbook with a smiling blonde chef on the cover and gorgeous food inside.

It was the kind of cookbook people in Connecticut display on their coffee tables and bore no resemblance to the sticky, flour dusted copy of Fannie Farmer on my kitchen counter. I wondered if cooking in Connecticut was really a different experience.

Does Martha Stewart disconnect the smoke alarm in her house before she broils the chicken? Has the fire department paid her a visit while she was blow-torching a lemon meringue pie?

When her husband asks, "What's in the potluck dinner?," does she answer, "You don't want to know."? Some of us whose Cuisinarts are still in their original box, want to know.

Does Miss Stewart have a dog shaped like a vacuum cleaner that eats mistakes? On the fourth day of Christmas, does her left-over turkey still resemble a centerpiece? Has she ever used Campbell's cream of mushroom soup and then told her mother-in-law she made the casserole from scratch? Some of us who make Snow Pudding from real snow want to know.

Since Martha signed on as a TV pitchperson for K-Mart, she seems more approachable—like a regular person with a four-burner stove and a linen closet full of poly-cotton.

Maybe now she'll loosen up. Perhaps she could start foot-noting her books with some of her failures, for those of us who hire a chimney sweep to clean our ovens.

Someone should talk to her agent. There's a market for disasters as well as triumphs. In fact, there's a market for a whole new type of cookbook: The Bungler's Cookbook.

To start, all recipes would be translated into English. No aioli when you mean garlic sauce, or meuniere for lemon butter. No whole corianders or crystallized mint leaves would be specified, only spices of two syllables or less; salt, pepper, thyme, sage, basil, dill.

Each listing of ingredients would contain only items normally found in a small-town refrigerator: cold mashed potatoes, ketchup. No cups of Mirepoix or half-tablespoons of chopped truffles or left-over fumet of blue she crab.

Standard pots and pans would be designated, along with one-blade appliances. Each recipe would not exceed one dishwasher load of spatulas, wire whisks or sticky bowls. The pages would be made out of sturdy, washable plastic so that the recipes can be used again.

A new category called Revenge Dinners would feature meals like Cusk Simmered in Castor Oil and Mango Monkfish. Local restaurants would be found in the index under Emergencies, along with Martha's home telephone number.

So what do you think, Martha? Those of us with sticky cookbooks would like to know.

LET'S SLICE OUR OWN CHEESE

**I** **HOPE** this won't be a "Hey buddy, can you spare a dime?" decade. I see the '90s as more of a "Could I borrow a cup of sugar?" era with folks spending more time at home cooking good, honest Fannie Farmer food the way they did years ago. Stuff like bread pudding. Not nouvelle cuisine from fancy cookbooks with lots of haut-y ingredients. We are going to have to toughen up. Think more economically.

I may not understand trillion dollar deficits, the Gross National Product or how we make money on wars, but I am beginning to grasp what is happening to our economy. Department stores are marking down their markdowns and advertising peculiar hours. These days, a 25-percent-off sale produces a yawn and 50 to 75 percent, a flicker of interest. We're only 25 percent away from looting.

It doesn't bode well. Gas is high and pork bellies are low. What's a person to do? I say, get back to basics. Slice our own cheese.

This solution occurred to me in the dairy department of the grocery store recently. I stood there surveying a sea of Swiss, Muenster, Mozzarella and Old English, all neatly presliced and individually wrapped, and asked myself: "Do I need this? Is my time so precious I need to buy sliced cheese?" The answer was no. I can learn to cut my own cheese again. And it's just the tip of the iceberg.

As a child, I was frugal. I discovered early on that you got more M&M's for your nickel when you bought them from a bin at W.T. Grant's than you did if you purchased the prepackaged brown bag. I know because I counted them. I was thrifty then. I can learn to be thrifty again.

It doesn't have to be painful. It can actually be healthy, beneficial—good for us. We should all tighten our belts; who amongst us doesn't need to lose a few pounds? Small, four-ounce portions will help us do it, by taking the bulge out of our waistlines and putting it where it belongs, in our wallets. By eliminating shrimp, lobster and filet mignon, we'll luxuriously lower our cholesterol.

Then we'll be fit to exercise. Forget fancy health clubs. The first step of our fitness program will be to take the first parking space we see. No driving around in circles and wasting gas. Eventually, we'll get in shape and be able to walk to the mall. Instead of "Fat and Happy," our motto will be "Cheap and Healthy."

We'll mend our ways and our socks too. No more discarding holey socks because our big toe sticks out. Scarlet O'Hara proved sewing can save the day by whipping up a gown out of green velvet drapes and bamboozling Rhett Butler. There's no question about it. Sewing circles will make a comeback, probably replacing lingerie parties.

Bartering will take the place of mindless shopping as a means of moving goods. You'll be able to trade your car, clothes, furniture or chores but not your spouse.

You must stay married. Stick it out till the year 2000. No one can afford a divorce now.

If you're not married, it's a good time to consider it. Then you'll be able to move in with your in-laws. A penny saved is a penny earned.

There may be hardships like drinking your coffee black but it's a time-honored tradition in difficult times. And changes in personal habits like dropping in on a friend at mealtime instead of dining out. Or ordering a wine that is customarily drunk in a doorway instead of the chateau's prize.

I'm not saying we should start lining our shoes with newspapers, but the days of conspicuous consumption are over. Unplug unnecessary appliances, turn the lights out when you leave a room and eat your toast raw. The handwriting is on the wall. It's time to start slicing our own cheese.

ALL YOU WANTED TO KNOW ABOUT QUARKS

OW can a word that sounds like a combination of a squawk and a quack be taken seriously? Quark. It seems like something a barnyard animal would say when you step on its tail. "Quark"? I say to my husband. "Subatomic particles," he answers.

I can't believe he understands what this quirky little word means.

"They've just found the top quark," I say, rattling the newspaper importantly. "You're probably familiar with up quark, down quark, charm quark, strange quark, and bottom quark. Now they've found the sixth one: top quark." I look over the top of the page, hoping to see a blank expression on his face. Instead, it's solemn and respectful. These names don't sound like six New Age dwarfs to him.

Not that my life is totally quarkless. I have heard of QuarkXpress, but I thought it was a computer program named by someone with a sense of whimsy.

I go back to studying the newspaper. "All matter in the universe is ultimately composed of infinitesimal particles called leptons and quarks."

I feel as if I'm reading the screenplay for "The Dark Crystal" or "The Hobbit." I don't understand what leptons are, either. The word has a friendly ring, though. If I were taking a foreign language exam, I'd take a stab at leprechaun as a translation.

But I digress. The story in the paper is about two different teams of physicists who were working away trying to find this top quark. Work, work, work. Then one of the teams found it last year. But, aha, they didn't have proof, which in this case would be a bunch of papers, because quarks are invisible. Now both teams have simultaneously announced that Eureka, they have found it.

To celebrate the discovery myself, I whipped out my un-abridged dictionary and looked up quark. "Arbitrary use of a word coined by James Joyce in 'Finnegans Wake.' Any of three hypothetical particles postulated as forming the building blocks of baryons and mesons and accounting in theory for their properties."

Building blocks of baryons. Very poetic. I flipped to the B's. Baryon: one of a class of heavy atomic particles, including the proton, neutron and the hyperon. This called for another flip. Meson: a mesotron, or in music, a tetrachord.

While I was at it, I looked up that cute little guy, lepton. Physicists must have their own private dictionaries, because mine said lepton is an ancient Greek coin of small value, or a modern one worth 1/100 of a drachma. Or maybe scientists think the universe is ultimately composed of tiny little coins.

Now that I had a lucid portrait of the top quark, I decided to take a quark awareness survey at work. "What's a quark?" I asked. No one hesitated for the slightest moment. "It's an as-tronomical term, having to do with stars and space." It has something to do with outer space, or a time-space-continuum thing." "It's either a black hole or atomic particle."

Personally, I thought they were outstanding answers.

With actual proof of the top quark, you may be wondering what the impact on our lives will be. Paul Grannis, a spokes-man for one of the discovery teams, says: It appears that we have observed the top quark. ... It is clearly a very highly sig-nificant result." Paul Tipton, a member of the other team, puts it this way: "It's certainly very important," giving physi-cists "much more confidence that the picture of how matter organizes itself" is correct.

So there you have it. All you ever wanted to know about quarks, nutshell version. And do you know what the best part is? It's fun to say. Try it. Quark!

REFRIGERATORS VERY REVEALING

BARBARA Walters could do a much more revealing interview if she cut out the chit-chat in the star's living room and crept into the kitchen with her film crew. I'd like to see the camera slowly pan up and down the shelves of the refrigerator. That's where a person's true self and innermost secrets are hiding.

I love to snoop in refrigerators.

Forget tarot cards, palm reading, handwriting analysis and psychoanalysis. I can tell you all about yourself, just by opening your refrigerator door. I am a diviner of food, a refrigerator interpreter, a toothsayer, so to speak.

A refrigerator is more honest than bookshelves, more intimate than clothes and more candid than a checkbook. You have to know a person well before you are allowed to open that door. My friend Gail is used to my peering in her refrigerator when I visit. Sure, I'm checking out what's to eat, but I'm also taking her pulse.

Has she been under a lot of pressure and too busy to shop? Are the shelves littered with furry nibs of this and wilted that? Is she into low-fat everything or premium ice cream? I inspect the egg bin and cheese drawer to see if she's sticking to a low cholesterol diet as she should.

A half-devoured chicken means she's been home; a doggie bag means she went out. I tick off the sensible food, convenience food and romantic food. I can tell if there's a tall, dark stranger in her life or if she's in a funk.

I'm surprised that psychiatrists don't make house calls. A patient can ramble on for hours talking about their traumas when all the doctor has to do is look into the person's refrigerator.

I have another friend who hates me to open her refrigerator. She acts as if I've caught her in the shower.

"I'll get the cream for your coffee," she says, leaping out of her kitchen chair.

"Sit down," I say. "I'm up, I'll get it." I know she would throw herself across the threshold of the refrigerator if she could, to keep me out.

"Wow! There's enough food in here for an army," I say, pushing deli cartons and mysterious foil-wrapped packages aside in my search for the Half and Half. "Are you having a party?"

"No." She smiles tightly. "My kids may drop by." She is embarrassed to have me see so much food in her refrigerator, but I understand. I'm a foodie, too.

A stuffed refrigerator is the equivalent of Fort Knox. Money in the bank. A security blanket.

Precision eaters are different. They plan each and every meal. There is no excess, no mismatches, no odd treats. They never wonder what they're going to eat. They live a life of control and regimentation.

A sense of adventure, health, laxity, politics, wealth, social image and personality are revealed behind the big white door. That's where I'd head if I were in a celebrity's home.

Does Liz Taylor have a hidden cache of Dove Bars and Lady Godiva chocolates in her freezer or is she sticking to her diet? Is that a decanter of grapefruit juice or something stronger?

Does Donald Trump's refrigerator contain flat champagne and dried-up caviar? Does Zsa Zsa keep her jewelry on ice or are those real carrots?

I'd guess Shirley MacLaine would stock wheat germ, tofu and alfalfa sprouts while her brother, Warren Beatty, probably keeps a bushel of oysters on ice at all times.

Does Cher eat long, thin food and Marlin Brando, round, plump food? These days, scientists take the notion seriously, that you are what you eat. I go one step further. I think you are your refrigerator.

INSIDER'S TIPS ON
YARD SALES

HAVING a yard sale is like declaring bankruptcy. You get 10 cents back on the dollar. A $40 shower curtain in its original wrapper will move for $4, regardless of how grotesque it is, but price it at $7 and you'll never get rid of it. Customers come from the farthest reaches of the earth to buy things cheap.

Never underestimate the appeal of the shabby, the rusty and the bent. Good condition means nothing. People are not interested in buying your latest mistakes; they're looking for frayed lampshades, pitted garden tools and two-legged Christmas tree stands. Save the new Cuisinart for your daughter's house warming.

Pricing is the most difficult part of a yard sale. The more attached you are to your old dependable lawn mower, the higher you want to price it. Something you don't like, like the French lace tablecloth your mother-in-law made, you'll price too low. Yard sale habituees thrive on this principle. Sentiment doesn't make cents. An impartial friend can help you even out your pricing.

Do not assume people will dicker. Many folks will browse past items that are priced too high. Remember you are trying to get rid of things; tag everything as low as you can. What you don't sell, you'll have to pack up and stuff back into the garage again. Be lenient. The bigger and bulkier the item, the better the deal should be.

If you advertise "No Early Birds," your driveway will be blocked two hours before you are ready. If you don't advertise "No Early Birds," people will be knocking at your door the night before. Decide which you prefer.

May is the prime month for yard sales. People are clawing at a chance to get out of the house. But take heed. Going to 10 yard sales does not bear any resemblance to having your own.

One has nothing in common with the other. The first few hours will rush by, then the entire day will drag. The day of the Midnight Sun will have new meaning. At two o'clock, you will think it's dinner time. It takes more than just having enough change on hand to have a successful yard sale; it takes style.

Do not dust, polish or shine anything. Let your customers envision the potential of waxing that cruddy chest of drawers. Create interesting uses for ordinary things. Display objects upside down as if you didn't know what they were. Say things like: "I don't know what this gizmo is, but it's been in the family for years." Hint at hidden values; be vague about ancestry. "Didn't whatshisname's rich grandfather own that desk?"

Offer to take returns. Most people are too lazy to come back, and it will help your credibility. Besides, they'll never find their way back, once you take the signs down.

Sell, sell, sell. Once someone picks something up, don't let them put it down. Invent an extra use for it. Do not set out a freebie bin. Customers are naturally suspicious and can be awfully picky about what they take for free. Instead, pile things on a table marked "Your Choice, 20 for $1."

If you are not sure whether you are a candidate for holding a yard sale, ask yourself the following question: Is my life one of simplicity, with a place for everything and everything in its place? Does my car fit into the garage? Do I have a house full of things I bought at yard sales that I have no use for? If you answered yes once, it's time to start writing your ad.

One further tip: try not to be depressed if someone with a jeweler's eyepiece snaps up all of Aunt Millie's costume jewelry in the first 10 minutes.

THE SIRENS OF WINTER

I must be a syndrome—an Irrational, Compulsive Seasonal Disorder that necessitates a dramatic and generally disastrous change in the filaments growing out of the top of my head. The disorder occurs in January and February. I find myself gravitating toward the brightly colored packages in the Hair Care aisle at the drugstore.

I finger bottles of henna, caress cartons of peroxide and contemplate instructions for root lifts and frothy perms. It is cabin fever of the hair.

Experience does not temper this condition. It matters not, that in previous years, I have transformed a normal head of hair into a frazzled ball of hemp or a tiger cat look-alike or Raggedy Anne wig. The sirens of winter call and I dance to their tune.

It is, after all, the time of year to officially turn over a new leaf. We are expected to change. Most resolve to be kinder, better, thinner or more fit. My resolution only takes two hours and lasts six months.

There is evidence to support my choice. In the movie "Punchline," Sally Fields decides that, if she is going to "go for it" as a comedian, she needs a new look. Michelle Pfeiffer discovers the same thing in "Married to the Mob." Even "Clara's Boy" gets a haircut.

We are hassled by magazines and movies to make ourselves over from stem to stern. We are shown how the dowdy and drab are transformed into the daring and the different. Like a voyeur with a Cinderella fetish, I study the "Before" and "After" photos wishing someone would wave the magic wand my way.

Will the right makeup turn a large beak into a button? Or the right hair color feel "worth it"? Enlightenment, success and happiness appear to be tied into changes in our appearance. I just want to know if a trip to the drugstore will do it.

And what about the person who's already lost 30 pounds, has short hair and knows how to pencil her eyebrows in? How will she get that promotion or the right guy?

How will she get through the next six weeks when there's no place to go with Irrational Compulsive Seasonal Disorder? Maybe there's a reverse solution, where you gain weight and let your hair grow to make your star rise.

I'd be impressed, for instance, if Oprah decided her teeth looked too big since she got skinny and she went back to snacking in flowing caftans. I wouldn't snicker if Arnold and Sylvester gave up pumping their pectorals and became couch potatoes who shopped in the portly department of Anderson Little. Jane Fonda would make me quite happy if she burned all her leotards and started producing bread-making videos.

I'd like to see wrong-season colors come back into vogue, and the makeup we wore in high school. And hear people say, "Wow. She changed back into herself!"

Then maybe I could put this bottle of henna back on the shelf. And begin working from the inside out.

TRUTH ABOUT EASTER BUNNY REVEALED

W E live with myths like Santa Claus and Cinderella, but of all of them, the Easter Bunny is the hardest one to swallow. Who can really imagine a big white rabbit skipping through town with a few thousand Easter baskets slung over his arm?

And, even if he did hop into your yard, how would he get into your house? There's no chimney for a bunny to slide down; no Easter sleigh powered by giant fuzzy chicks. And where did the big fellow get all those jellybeans, cream-filled eggs and cellophane grass, huh?

Pink, yellow and purple spring flowers make sense and maybe even egg hunts. They probably have something to do with fecundity, signs of rebirth and good luck. But how did the rest of this stuff get by us?

"I have no idea," said my friend Gail, when I asked her about the origin of the Easter Bunny.

"It's based on some sort of Nordic or Celtic tradition," said my husband.

"We don't have an Easter Bunny," said my neighbor Tina. "It's not a Greek tradition."

"I'm trying to think back," said my 87-year-old mother-in-law. "I don't recall. But we had those marshmallow things."

The Easter Bunny wasn't even listed in my Webster's Unabridged Dictionary, which contains 3000 illustrations and full-color maps of the world.

In desperation, I called the U.S. Department of Agriculture. Maybe rabbits were considered farm animals. The phone rang a long time. Finally someone answered and apologized. They were in the midst of a study of homosexual sheep.

"For purely economical reason," the man said. "You wouldn't want to pay $4000 for a breeding ram that wasn't interested in ewes, would you?"

When I finally got to ask my question, he said, "Easter Bunny? Nope. Don't think we've ever studied him."

I decided to try the CIA. They probably have a file on the Tooth Fairy.

"Cuba, David Duke, Easter Bunny. Yep we've got him," I was told. After I promised I wouldn't reveal my sources, I got the lowdown.

The Easter Bunny came about because of one Howard "Nutsy" Hallmark. "Howe Nutsy" as his brother called him. He was a good man, a bit of a dreamer, who wrote verse in his spare time and ran the local basket shop next to the post office.

Howe Nutsy's wife drove him crazy with her cooking. "Try this," she'd say, as soon as he got in the door at night, waving a huge platter of pink-and-white marshmallow rabbits under his nose.

"Look what I invented," she'd exclaim the next day. "Chocolate cream eggs!" Howe Nutsy didn't know how to respond. He wasn't much of a sweet eater himself.

I have to devise a plan, he said to himself. I love my wife and want to make her happy but I can't go on feeding the poor beagle all the things she creates. The truth was, that as much as he loved his wife, he loved his beagle more.

So Howe Nutsy began creeping around the neighborhood leaving baskets of goodies on people's doorsteps.

"I'll just take this whole batch of goodies to work with me for lunch," he'd tell his wife, then slip into the costume he made.

The bunny suit was a stroke of genius, he thought. If he got caught, no one would recognize him, hee, hee. For fun, he left a card with some of his verse on it.

Soon the town was in an uproar. Folks who didn't find baskets at their door were jealous of those who did. They wouldn't admit it though. Instead they bought one at Howe Nutsy's store and pretended they had found it.

Once someone caught Howe Nutsy nibbling on a marsh-mallow chick. "Do you have any more of those?" he was asked.

"Why yes, I do," he answered and a new business was born. "How about a nice little card to go with them?"

THE MORPHIC
ANOMALY PRINCIPLE

IT'S not that things don't fit in the beginning. No. When you buy a road map, it is neatly folded into an unobtrusive package. Fits right into the glove compartment. That is, until you use it. Then, whammo. It grows like a pot of popping corn. Even when you fold it back on the creases carefully, it is still double its original size. A fistful of map.

Well, guys who were in charge of maps in the army, architects, puzzle designers, and math professors can do a reasonable job of refolding, but not your run-of-the-mill citizen. Nine out of 10 people have the dexterity of a stonecrab. I think it was a big mistake when they abandoned cloth maps that rolled up.

Who makes these things and how do they get away with it? Take fitted sheets. They fit fine when you take them out of the cellophane package. Slip right on the mattress, they do. Very civilized, until you wash them. Then things change.

The first two corners go on as you remember. The third may need a little lift of the mattress. The fourth requires the strength of a Sumo wrestler, the agility of an acrobat and the patience of Mother Teresa. At that point, you read the little tag to see if you bought the right size. It says, "Preshrunk. Queen." It should say, "Not recommended for people who change the linens alone."

The moment a seal is broken on a container, it enters an altered state that cannot be explained. It happens to peanut butter jars, mayonnaise jars, ketchup bottles and anything plastic that contains something fizzy. It's not that the caps and lids are damaged. If they were, the item could be returned to the store. It is something in the design that requires a person to have the concentration of a magician, the stealth of an envelope steamer and the deftness of a safecracker.

What once seemed squarish when you bought it, gets roundish when you own it. Keys reject locks; electric plugs fight sockets. But no one complains.

We know a house can warp and heave so that doors don't close or windows won't open. It makes sense to us because there's a perfectly reasonable explanation. If you open a drawer and don't close it right away, the wood molecules swell up due to atmospheric pressure and you won't be able to slide it back in place till the next full moon. It's normal.

Nature may throw a little dust in our eyes, but Nature is not a charlatan like some people. It's probably our own fault. We were all lying around on our couches watching Bill Cosby and eating Jello while significant breakthroughs were being made in the marketplace. The development of the Morphic Anomaly Principle or something New Wave.

Have you ever noticed how clothes fit differently in a store? "This is comfortable," you say, turning to and fro, in front of the dressing room mirror. They you get it home and it cuts your circulation off.

What do you do? You feel guilt. Was it the cherry cheesecake I ate last night? Was I feeling too optimistic and thin when I bought it? Was there a rare planetary alignment with Venus, Neptune and Pluto forming a crescent with the moon that pulled in such a way that the article of clothing actually felt fine at that moment and won't again until the identical formation occurs in the universe—roughly 9.3 years from now?

Is there a new species of fabric mite that can condense clothing without leaving tell-tale holes, while a person sleeps?

Could it be true that human bodies contract to half-a-size smaller in the hermetically sealed atmosphere of the mall? That air in a retail store is different from the air in an average home? And stores crank up the air compression when they run a sale, causing customers to stock up on clothing that is two sizes too small?

My own theory is that manufacturers have developed a new fabric softener-type ingredient that allows a garment to stretch once, when you try it on, and then snaps back to its original size, when you get it home.

People used to say, "If the shoe fits, wear it." Now all you hear is, "Buyer beware." The masters of the marketplace are loathe to discuss it. The secret of Why Things Don't Fit will probably die with them and become one of the wonders of the world like the Egyptian Tombs, Stonehenge and where the funny little screws come from that appear from thin air on your kitchen counter.

ABOUT THE AUTHOR

Stephanie Foster has been writing her popular column "Just Looking" since 1989, when it first appeared in the Harwich Oracle. Since then, she has won numerous awards for humor, including two first places from the New England Press Association. A devoted gardener and photographer, she lives on Cape Cod, Massachusetts with her husband Frank, who is a commercial photographer, and her two Maine Coon cats.